AUNT EDNA

and The Lightning Rock

by C. A. HOCKING

Book 1 of the Aunt Edna Stories

An Australian Children's Fable of
Weirdness and Wonder!

DEDICATION

For Hayden, Alia, Alex and Ruby,
Mitchell, Jaimee, Tiana, Kelsey and Ainslee

With many thanks to my Splendid Editors, Charlie Karlsen, Meg Birrell and Elizabeth England;
and to my Chief Test Reader, Ainslee Henman,
for her intelligent and insightful input.

Copyright © 2019 C. A. HOCKING
ISBN: 9780975849040
All rights reserved. Without limiting the rights under copyright above, no part of this publication shall be reproduced, stored in or introduced into a retrieval system, or transmitted in any form or by any means (electronic, mechanical, photocopying, recording or otherwise), without the prior permission of the copyright owner of this book.
Enquiries should be addressed to the
author at **www.cahocking.com**
Cover art by **BrillianBookCovers**

CHAPTER 1

A Letter and Buckets of Money

Aunt Edna wasn't much to look at. She was about five feet three inches tall with lumpy arms and fat legs, but when she crossed her arms and stuck out her chin, which happened when she was annoyed, she looked very imposing and nobody could ever agree on whether she was tall or short. Most people thought she was about seventy years old, which is very old to an eleven year old, but quite young to a ninety year old. Those people were all wrong as she was much, much, much older than seventy and that was because she was an Eternal. She'd become an Eternal after being struck by blue lightning when she tried calling up her husband's ghost on the Lightning Rock. But more of that later.

She had short wispy grey hair that she cut with a rusty old pair of sewing scissors, and lots of friendly wrinkles which made her face look like she was smiling even when she wasn't. Her large blue eyes looked even larger because she wore thick spectacles with black frames that had been stuck together with bandaids every time she broke them. She broke them often. She used to forget where she left her glasses, which was usually on the kitchen chair and, of course, she always sat on them. She would know that she'd sat on them because she would hear them crack, but she never really felt them as she had a large, soft bum that was as good as any well padded cushion. She also had a large soft belly and big saggy boobs.

Aunt Edna liked to wear brown dresses with gold buttons down the front and a wide black belt buckled between her big belly and big boobs. To match her brown dresses, she wore brown elastic sided work boots and brown socks. She liked brown because it didn't show the dirt. She wore a stained old Akubra hat with frayed edges that hung on a hook by the door when she was inside, but always stayed on her head when she was outside. It never blew off, no matter how strong the wind was. She thought she looked very smart indeed.

When Aunt Edna smiled, her eyes twinkled and her teeth showed. They were very straight white teeth because they weren't really old lady teeth. They were false teeth which are called dentures. She'd had dentures a very long time and kept wearing them down. A dentist made her a new pair every ten years or so. Dentures are fine until you eat crisp apples or toffee and then they tend to get stuck in the food. When that happened, Aunt Edna would take her teeth out, prise the food off them and pop them back in. Sometimes, if she got very excited about something, they would shoot out of her mouth. She was very good at catching them before they hit the ground, but it was best not to stand too close to her when that happened. Getting hit by a pair of flying teeth was no fun at all.

When she laughed, her teeth would rattle together. Aunt Edna was famous for her laugh. It was loud and cackley and always made people around her laugh too, even though they were not sure what they were laughing at. Laughter is like a cold, it is catching.

Aunt Edna lived in a big old bluestone house on a farm. There were many old stone buildings around the house - stables and shearing sheds and equipment sheds - but they'd been empty for a long time. The farm was called Hopperfield Station and was about half an hour's drive out of town. The town was called Hopperfield after Aunt Edna's grandfather, Thomas Hopperfield Senior who was a pioneer in the area. It was about an hour's drive east of Adelaide in South Australia.

The farm was fifty thousand acres, which is not so big in Australia, but is very big in other parts of the world. When she was a young woman, wheat grew and sheep grazed in large paddocks and horses filled the stables and exercise yards, but there hadn't been any wheat or sheep or horses on the farm for nearly a hundred years. Instead of farming, Aunt Edna spent a lot of time planting native tree seedlings in the huge paddocks so that every year the farm looked more and more like the bush instead of a farm. She did that because of a trade she'd made with the Lightning Rock.

When people first met Aunt Edna, they sometimes thought she was a little vague, a little deaf, even a little stupid because she seemed to stare off into space quite a bit, didn't always hear what was said to her and sometimes talked to herself. But they quickly discovered she was as sharp as a tack and didn't miss a thing. She knew what was happening around the district without anyone telling her. She knew when someone was sick or going through hard times or short of money or falling in love or falling out of love. She would turn up at a neighbouring farmer's house with a broccoli casserole or money or advice or sometimes just a shoulder to cry on.

Everyone knew she was a little odd, but everyone loved her. She was always called Aunt Edna even though she was nobody's aunt. No one was sure why they called her Aunt Edna, they just did. She was very special.

Aunt Edna also knew secrets that no one else even knew were secrets. She knew about bored ghosts and fat vampires, about werewolves with fleas and banshees with sore throats, about patient zombies and fat lazy dogs and grumpy old cats and big hairy spiders and timid snakes. Because she knew the truth about these things, Aunt Edna wasn't afraid of anything. Or she thought she wasn't afraid of anything.

Until she got the letter.

It was November which is the end of spring in Australia and it was already very hot. She'd spoken to the Great Smoking Beastie in the shed and told it they needed to go into town to shop and collect her mail from the Post Office. The Great Smoking Beastie was really an old 1934 Ford ute with a noisy engine that belched great gusts of black smoke. In Australia, a ute is like a car at the front with a seat for the driver and passenger, but like a truck at the back that can carry things like bales of hay and toolboxes. This particular ute looked rather peculiar. It was dented all over, had rusty patches around the wheels, scratches in the faded blue paint and two broken headlights that shone in the dark, despite having no globes in them. Aunt Edna knew it had a mind of its own as it seemed to frown when it did not want to do something and smile when it did. It had to be in the right mood to go and, fortunately for Aunt Edna, it was in a good mood on this day and agreed to take her into town.

She fed the Great Smoking Beastie some petrol from the pump next to the shed, gave it a friendly little pat on the bonnet, waited a moment while it started up, sat behind the wheel and let it drive her into town in a cloud of black smoke and red dust. She took a book from her big old brown handbag, leaned it on the steering wheel and read it while the Great Smoking Beastie veered from one side of the red dirt road to the other, trying to avoid the potholes. Aunt Edna appreciated the Great Smoking Beastie's efforts to avoid the potholes as it made the journey much less bumpy.

When they stopped outside the Post Office, Aunt Edna waited for the engine to turn itself off and got out. She stretched her legs and wiped the red dust from her face and glasses. A neatly dressed lady walked past, smiled and said, "Good morning, Aunt Edna. How are you today?"

"I'm as I always am, Olive. And you?"

Olive said, "I am well, thank you. Will we see you at the Christmas Dance next month?"

"Next month? Is it almost next month already?" Aunt Edna brushed the dust from her dress and it settled in a dry puddle around her brown boots. "Yes, I'll be there. Broccoli scones?"

"Broccoli scones would be lovely, thank you, Aunt Edna,"

"Broccoli scones it will be, then. See you there." Aunt Edna smiled with her smiling wrinkled face and went into the Post Office.

Gerald, the Postmaster, hailed Aunt Edna with a hearty, "Aunt Edna! I hoped we'd see you today."

"Well, of course, dear boy. It's the first of the month ... isn't it?"

"It's the middle of the month, but I knew you'd remember eventually."

"The middle of the month? Oh ... hhmm ... well ... doesn't matter."

"No, doesn't matter," Gerald said. "You always forget and it always takes you a couple of weeks to remember. But here you are."

"Yes, here I am. I am here, am I not?" Aunt Edna looked down at herself. "Yes, I'm definitely here."

"I've got your mail ready."

"Good boy. Just the usual?"

"Mostly. Rates, electricity, telephone. And a letter. Got your debit card?"

"The card. Oh ... yes ... the card." Aunt Edna fished around in her handbag which had many things in it, so many that she had long forgotten what was there, until she felt the flat plastic card. She blew the dust off it and handed it to Gerald. Aunt Edna didn't understand how the small piece of plastic worked. "I don't like the card thingy. It's not proper money."

"I know you don't, Aunt Edna, but you know you can't use the old bank books any more. It has to be the card." Gerald handed her a bundle of mail. "Now remember what I taught you. Open your bills first."

Aunt Edna opened each one and passed them to Gerald. He smoothed them out and put them in a pile next to the computer. Just when Aunt Edna thought she'd opened all her mail, there at the bottom of the pile was ... the letter. It looked different from the other envelopes and seemed to glow and vibrate a little in her hand. She held it up. "What's this?"

Gerald took the envelope. "Nice paper. Gold embossed address. Quality." He turned it over to read the sender's address. "It's from a lawyer in Sydney."

"Well, that's just silly. I don't know anyone in Sydney. And my lawyers are in Adelaide. Why would a lawyer in Sydney write to me?"

"Better open it and find out while I put your bills through. Do you remember your PIN?"

"PIN? Why do I need a pin? Have I lost a button?" She looked down at the buttons on her dress, but couldn't see any missing.

Gerald sighed. They went through this every time Aunt Edna came to town. "No, your PIN - your Personal Identification Number. Remember? It could be your birthday or some number that means something to you."

"Oh, that. The secret number."

"That's right, the secret number. I'll look away and you punch in your secret number. Tell me when you are done."

Gerald waved Aunt Edna's card over a little machine, tapped a few keys and looked away. Aunt Edna narrowed her eyes, looked around her suspiciously even though there was no one else in the Post Office, and punched 1840 into the machine. 1840 was the year of her birth. Gerald said, "Done?"

"Yes."

"Good." Gerald hit the Enter button and proceeded to pay Aunt Edna's bills. While he did so, she sat on a chair and opened her letter. It read:

> "Dear Mrs Toddleby,
>
> Our firm represents the interests of Isobel Hopperfield whose parents both died in a tragic road accident during a holiday in England six months ago. Isobel was not with them at the time.
>
> After extensive investigations, a will was located belonging to Isobel's great-grandfather, Thomas Hopperfield, who named his sister, Mrs Edna Toddleby of Hopperfield Station in South Australia as an heir to his substantial fortune.
>
> We have learned that Hopperfield Station is still owned by an Edna Toddleby who we believe may be a granddaughter of

the original Edna Toddleby. If so, you may be the only living relative of Isobel Hopperfield and may wish to be involved with her future welfare.

We await your response to this correspondence.

Yours Sincerely

Jonathon Hamble"

Aunt Edna looked up from the letter and said, "Well I never."

Gerald stopped what he was doing. "Anything wrong, Aunt Edna?"

"I think I've got a niece."

Gerald looked surprised. "A niece? I didn't know you had a brother or sister."

"Oh yes. A brother. Thomas. But he died in Africa a long time ago."

"Africa?"

"Yes. Africa. He went there during the drought ..."

"The drought we've just been through?"

"Oh no, the Big Drought. A long, long time ago. Before you were born. The crops died and everything turned to dust. It lasted for more than twenty years. Thomas decided being a farmer was too hard and then he heard about diamonds being discovered in Africa, so he thought he'd try his luck there. He bought some land, started digging and found so many diamonds, it made him very, very rich. He never came home again, poor dear, got typhoid or some such thing and died quite young. And when he died, he left the diamond mine to me."

"Diamond mine?" Gerald was looking very surprised indeed. "You owned a diamond mine?"

"Still do. That's why I'm so rich. I've got diamonds coming out of my ears and buckets of money.

"Well I never." Gerald was staring at her with his mouth open. "I knew you were well off, but I thought it was because of Hopperfield Station."

"The farm? Oh no, dear boy. I haven't made any money from that for many years. No, it's the diamonds, you see. I used to get a cheque every six months from the company that manages the mine, but now they just pay it into my account and send me a statement telling me how much I have."

Gerald held up Aunt Edna's debit card. "This account?"

"Yes. I only ever had one account."

"Are you worth ... a lot?"

"Millions, dear boy, millions! I sit in my house at Hopperfield Station and someone I've never met just keeps giving me money."

Gerald was looking at Aunt Edna's debit card with awe. She put her hand out for it. "Have you finished paying my bills?"

"Yes. Oh yes." He handed her the debit card, which she dropped back into the shambles that was her old brown handbag. "And now you have a niece?"

Aunt Edna looked at the letter again. "Well, it seems she's my brother's son's son's daughter. Goodness, I never knew he had a son. Or a grandson. He wasn't a letter writer and I didn't know much about his life in Africa. All I got was a letter from a lawyer much like this one, telling me he'd died and left me the diamond mine. It didn't mention a family. So ... if she's my brother's son's son's daughter, does that make her my niece?"

Gerald thought for a moment. "That makes her your great great niece."

"Is that as good as a niece?"

"Just as good. It's a descendant, Aunt Edna. You have a descendant."

Aunt Edna's eyes opened wide with surprise. "Goodness. I've never had one of those before. I thought I was the last one." She sat back in the chair and said again, "Well I never."

"How old is your great great niece?"

"Oh." Aunt Edna scanned the letter again. "It doesn't say."

Gerald gave her a strange look. "If she is the daughter of your brother's grandson ... how old are you?"

"Me? Goodness, I'm not sure. I never was very good with numbers."

"What year were you born?"

"Oh, I don't remember. I was only a baby at the time."

"I've been here for over forty years and do you know that you look exactly the same now as you did when I first came to Hopperfield?"

"Well, they say people are living longer, don't they?" Aunt Edna looked at the letter again and changed the subject. "Oh dear. What if Isobel is just a baby? I wouldn't know what to do with a baby."

"Are you going to reply to the letter?"

"Yes. I shall write to them and tell them Isobel is most certainly my family."

Gerald stapled receipts to Aunt Edna's bills and passed them to her. "Do you want to write the letter while you are here? I know it's quite a journey to Hopperfield Station. Might save you another trip just to post a letter."

"Jolly good idea. I'll do that now."

Gerald gave Aunt Edna pen, paper and envelope and she wrote to the lawyer:

"Dear Mr Jonathon Hamble,

I am indeed a relative of Isobel Hopperfield. I will be happy to take responsibility for her welfare. Please write to me again and tell me what plans you would like me to make for her. And by the way, how old is Isobel?

Yours Sincerely

Edna Olive Margaret Mae Amelia Louise Hopperfield Toddleby."

Aunt Edna put the letter into an envelope. Gerald wrote the lawyer's address on it, stuck on a stamp and popped it into the mail bag.

Aunt Edna then went to the grocery store, bought some supplies, threw them into the back of the Great Smoking Beastie and began the journey home.

And that was when she began to feel afraid. A niece? What on earth would she do with a niece?

CHAPTER 2

A Fat Manila Envelope and a Panic Attack

Two weeks later, Aunt Edna had a visitor. She knew she had a visitor long before the visitor arrived because Diggidydog, who spent most of his time asleep on the front veranda, raised his head, barked and wagged his tail. Diggidydog was a fat old Labrador who was once gold and full of bounce, but now he was mostly grey and completely toothless. He napped a lot on the front veranda and didn't like to be bothered unless it was for something to eat. His favourite food was fried mince meat, gravy and mashed broccoli. He didn't need teeth for that. He was very, very old and would be so forever, because he had also been struck by blue lightning on the Lightning Rock at the same time as Aunt Edna.

Diggidydog only ever barked for two reasons. One was if a visitor was approaching and then he barked with a laughing bark and thumped his tail on the veranda without getting up. When Aunt Edna heard that bark, she knew she had about twenty minutes to tidy herself up for the visitor, because it took twenty minutes from the time they passed through the farm gates until they reached the house. The visitor had to drive along a dirt track between two rows of very old gum trees with branches that met high over the track. Even on the hottest days, the track was shady and much cooler than the nearby paddocks.

The other reason Diggidydog barked was when a Red Snow Storm approached from the north. They weren't really snow storms, they were red dust storms, but the dust was so thick that you couldn't see in front of you and it was like being in a blizzard, only redder, hotter and dustier. There were ordinary brown dust storms, too, but the red ones were quite different. They carried more than dust, but only dogs, cats and Aunt Edna knew that. When a Red Snow Storm was bearing down on Hopperfield Station, Diggidydog would bark sharply to alert Aunt Edna. Then he would stand on the veranda barking loudly with his eyes open and ears listening for the whisper of vampire wings on the wind. Grumblebumkin would come outside to check if there was a full moon, just in case the werewolves were about as well.

Grumblebumkin was a bad tempered old ginger tabby cat, so feared by werewolves that Aunt Edna knew she had nothing to worry about as long as he was on the case. Where once he had been bright orange with white stripes, his stripes were now grey and a dull rusty colour, but he still had wild green eyes and long thick black whiskers that made him look every bit as fearsome as he was. Grumblebumkin had been draped around Aunt Edna's neck, which was still his favourite place to rest, when she'd been struck by blue lightning on the Lightning Rock, so he would be old forever like Diggidydog.

On this day, Diggidydog gave the visitor's bark, closed his eyes and went back to sleep. There was nothing else for him to do. Grumblebumkin came out onto the veranda to see who was coming because cats are curious by nature. He sat with his ginger and grey tail wrapped elegantly around his ginger and grey body and waited.

Aunt Edna was in the kitchen making broccoli scones for the summer dance when she heard the visitor's bark. She knew she had twenty minutes before the visitor arrived, so she carried on with what she was doing which was looking for an extra baking tray. It was somewhere in the kitchen, she knew that. All she had to do was keep looking and it would turn up. Things she looked for always turned up in the end.

The house had been built just before Aunt Edna was born, with four big windows across the front, a wide veranda that wrapped all the way around to the back, and a long central passage with twelve large airy rooms opening off it. It had once been quite grand, but now it looked a little tired and shabby. The window frames needed painting, the slate tiles on the veranda were cracked and the iron roof was rusty.

Every room in the house was jammed full of furniture and clutter, for Aunt Edna never threw anything out that might one day be useful. It could have been a terrible mess, but Aunt Edna kept it dusted, clean and tidy. She knew where everything was, or she thought she did, but of course she didn't. There was just too much of it to keep track of and she spent a lot of time looking for things.

The kitchen at the back of the house was her favourite room. It had lots of rickety cupboards and sagging shelves jammed full of bits and bobs. Barking Wood Stove sat next to a modern electric stove, but Aunt Edna didn't like the modern stove. She always burnt the scones in that. She much preferred Barking Wood Stove with the fire burning away cheerfully inside it, even in the summer time. Barking Wood Stove understood what she needed and never ever burnt anything. If Aunt Edna forgot she'd put something in the oven, which she did sometimes, the oven would simply emit a loud

WOOF, cough out a puff of smoke and stop cooking.

However, Barking Wood Stove made the kitchen very hot in summer. It was fine during the winter and Aunt Edna liked to eat at the long kitchen table then, but in summer she ate at a small table and chair on the back veranda under the old pepper tree where it was much cooler.

While she was looking for the extra baking tray, she glanced through the back window and saw it on the little table on the veranda. Then she remembered she'd used it as a tray for her morning tea with Bert inside the freezer at the end of the veranda. It was a very big industrial freezer, so big you could open the door and walk right inside it. Although it was rather old and rusty around the edges, it still worked and that was all that mattered. It was the first big freezer to be installed anywhere in the district, back in 1910 when people had ice chests and cellars to keep their food fresh. It had run off an old generator before Aunt Edna got electricity connected up in 1959. If the power failed, and it did sometimes, the old generator would kick in with a loud rattle and keep everything from thawing out.

Aunt Edna was very particular about keeping the freezer going. She kept all her meat, fish fingers, frozen vegetables and her husband, Bert, in the freezer. Bert had a screened-off section all to himself at the back of the freezer. He sat in a wheelchair in his blue striped pyjamas with big dark sunglasses covering his eyes, his hands folded in his lap, dead and frozen solid. He had sat in that wheelchair since 1910. He wore the big dark sunglasses because being frozen made his eyes go black and Aunt Edna didn't like the way that looked, so she'd put the sunglasses on him in 1962. She thought they suited him.

Aunt Edna went outside to collect her baking tray. She heard the sound of blowflies buzzing around and waved them towards the Spider House behind the back veranda. It had once been the old washhouse. After the new laundry had been installed inside the house, there was no more use for the old washhouse. It had become dusty and full of cobwebs. That's when Aunt Edna realised it was the perfect place for spiders to live. If Aunt Edna found a spider in her house, she ordered it into the Spider House. Spiders were all good and well, but they should know their place. A house for her and a house for them. That's the way she liked it.

Aunt Edna picked up the baking tray and looked up at the Lightning Rock behind the house. It was the only hill for miles around and dominated the landscape like a pyramid. It was covered in gum trees and scrub and when you followed the track up the hill, you came to the waterhole halfway up and then the Lightning Rock at the very top. When the sun was shining, the Lightning Rock gleamed like a shiny, flat black hat on top of the hill.

On gloomy wet days, it looked like a big blackhead that needed squeezing. Today it gleamed and there were no storm clouds above it. All was well.

Aunt Edna took the baking tray inside and removed her apron. The twenty minutes was almost up. She wiped the flour from her face and went outside as a red Post Office van stopped by the front steps.

Gerald got out. He had a fat manila envelope in his hand and he waved it at her. "Registered mail, Aunt Edna."

"For me? Oh my, who would be sending me registered mail?"

"It's from that same lawyer in Sydney. I thought it might be important and I knew you weren't due to come to town today, so I brought it out to you."

"Dear boy, that is very kind of you."

"Just sign here and it's all yours." Gerald handed her a form.

Aunt Edna signed the form and took the envelope. "Come in out of the heat, Gerald. There's iced tea in the fridge and I've made fresh broccoli scones."

The house was cool inside until they got to the kitchen. As they entered, Barking Wood Stove suddenly belched a loud WOOF, blew smoke across the room and Aunt Edna knew the scones were done. She thanked Barking Wood Stove by tossing another log into the fire, then took the scones out, put them on a cooling rack and said, "It's too hot in here, we'll have morning tea in the dining room." She led the way to one of the cluttered front rooms and sat Gerald down at the big mahogany dining table. In a moment, she had a jug of iced liquorice tea, green scones, yellow jam and blue cream in front of him. He tucked in while she sat down and opened the envelope. Gerald sighed with pleasure. He was always amazed at how good Aunt Edna's broccoli scones tasted and her food was always colourful, although a little mysterious.

Aunt Edna removed the documents from the manila envelope and spread them out on the table. "Let's see what we have here. There's a letter. Dear Mrs Toddleby ... blah blah blah ... goodness, why can't lawyers just say something in plain words. Oh. My niece Isobel is eleven years old. Well I never. Eleven. That's better than a baby I suppose. Babies keep you awake at night. And better than sixteen or seventeen. Teenage girls can be such a pest. I know I was. More blah blah blah ... Isobel goes to the best private boarding school in Sydney, the term is due to finish in ... hhmmm, two weeks ... they break for the summer holidays over Christmas ... blah blah blah ... can she come here for the holidays ... they ask me to consider being her legal guardian ... they have gathered references from several people in this district ... oh my ... they've been speaking to the Reverend, the Mayor, the Police Sergeant, the school principal ... my, my, my, they have been busy ... apparently I'm a pillar of the community, a woman of substantial reputation and means, and considered a fine candidate to raise Isobel ..."

Aunt Edna stopped suddenly and looked up at Gerald with startled blue eyes. "Raise Isobel?" She put the letter to one side and looked at the rest of the paperwork with some confusion. "Gerald, can you make sense of any of this?" She handed it all to Gerald who quickly scanned the documents.

"This one is a Power of Attorney, this one is for Legal Guardianship, this one is for access to Isobel's trust fund for her personal, living and education needs, and these others ... well, basically Aunt Edna, they are handing Isobel over to you. And it says here that Isobel will be delivered to you in two weeks when the school term finishes if you return all the completed documents."

"Goodness!"

Aunt Edna and Gerald stared at each other.

"Yes. Goodness!" Gerald agreed.

"Two weeks?"

"Two weeks, Aunt Edna."

"Oh dear."

"Will you write to tell them you'd rather she didn't come here?"

Aunt Edna replied without hesitation. "Oh no. She should definitely come here. Poor little girl. She has no one else in the world. And she's a Hopperfield. Here is where she should be." Then she paused and said uncertainly, "But..."

"But?"

Aunt Edna looked around her at the cluttered room full of too much beautiful old furniture and too many pictures on the walls and cracked paint and peeling wallpaper and possum wee stains on the ceiling and tatty curtains at the windows and had a panic attack. Her eyebrows went up and down, her teeth rattled, her eyes looked this way and that. She jumped up and to began to spin around in circles, her arms waving about and her feet prancing up and down.

"Oh my oh my oh my ... what do eleven year old girls EAT? What do they WEAR? What do they DO? Where will she SLEEP? Which bedroom shall I put her in? There are so many. Should she sleep in a small bed or a big bed? Where are all my guest sheets? I haven't had anyone stay in this house for over fifty years. What if all the guest sheets have gone mouldy? What if ... what if ... oh my oh my oh my ..."

Gerald got up and began patting Aunt Edna gently on the back. "It's alright, Aunt Edna, it's alright. Just breathe slowly, have a sip of tea, breathe again. Everything's going to be alright."

Aunt Edna stopped spinning, took a deep breath and sat back in her chair.

Gerald poured another glass of iced tea for Aunt Edna and looked around him. "It won't be too hard to sort everything out here. But you might need some help."

"Help?" Aunt Edna took a slurpy swig of tea and sighed gratefully. The panic attack was over.

"Yes. You've helped everyone in the district at one time or another, including me. Why, when my eldest boy was sick, you arranged for him to see the specialist in Adelaide in one day when our own doctor couldn't get him in for a month. I don't know how you did it, but it saved his life."

Aunt Edna looked at Gerald sympathetically. "That was easy. I just paid him double his fee up front. Money can be very useful at times." She thought for a moment. "You have three grown up daughters, Gerald. What did they need when they were eleven years old?"

"Well, considering she's recently lost her parents, what Isobel will need is love, reassurance and security."

"Yes, yes, that goes without saying. But what will she NEED?"

Gerald smiled. He understood the question. "Well, she'll need sturdy clothes for the farm. If she's a city girl, she probably doesn't have those. She'll need good food, a comfortable bed, an understanding ear and a vigilant eye.

It's a tricky stage for a girl, being eleven. They need love and guidance at the same time. But why don't we just start with where she's going to sleep? The rest will come a bit at a time."

"Sleep. Yes. Well. There's my brother's old room, it's just as it was the day he left. And my parents' old room. And my grandparents' old room. And the first guest room. And the second guest room..."

"OK. We'll stop there. Let's just get this paperwork done today and I'll arrange for some help to sort out the rest. Alright?"

"Very well."

"May I use your phone to let the Post Office know I'll be out here for awhile?"

"Of course. It's right there." Aunt Edna pointed to a big black phone with a round metal disc on it. Gerald looked at it and smiled.

"I haven't seen one of those since the 1950's," he said. "You should update your phone, Aunt Edna, maybe even get a mobile phone. There is a new tower being built in Hopperfield. It'll be finished by Christmas. You would get good reception out here."

"What, one of those little baby phones? I'd need a magnifying glass to find it, let alone see the numbers on it. And this one works just fine. Why replace something that works?"

"Why indeed," Gerald agreed.

Aunt Edna and Gerald spent the next few hours working through the paperwork from the Sydney lawyers. Every so often, when Gerald was reading a bit out to her, Aunt Edna would tilt her head to one side as if listening to something Gerald couldn't hear, then nod and say, "Yes, yes, I understand." It seemed like a long day. When Gerald left, Aunt Edna felt quite overwhelmed and needed something ordinary to do, so she went into the kitchen and baked another two hundred broccoli scones.

CHAPTER 3

Helping Hands and a Slap-Up Barbecue

Two days later, Aunt Edna was going through her many cupboards looking for the guest sheets she knew had to be somewhere, when she heard Diggidydog's laughing bark. Someone was coming. She went into the bathroom to tidy herself up, then stopped to listen again. Diggidydog was still barking his laughing bark. That was unusual. She went out onto the front veranda and there, coming up her long driveway, was a convoy of cars, utes and trucks.

It was the help that Gerald had said he would arrange. The whole District of Hopperfield had answered his call.

The front driveway quickly filled with vehicles and many helpers made their way into the house. So many helpers that every room was filled with people asking, "Aunt Edna, where do you want this moved?" "Aunt Edna, what's in this cupboard?" "Aunt Edna, can we vacuum this rug and polish the floor underneath?" "Aunt Edna, which room is your niece going to sleep in?" "Aunt Edna, can we put some new curtains up at this window?" So many questions, so many helpers. Aunt Edna felt herself spinning around and around in circles, trying to answer everyone at once.

Gerald saw Aunt Edna's confusion and called out, "Stop!" Everyone stopped. "Let's get organised," he said. "We'll do one room at a time. We'll start with the room Aunt Edna's niece is going to sleep in. And her name is Isobel. Isobel Hopperfield." He turned to Aunt Edna. "Have you decided which room Isobel will sleep in, Aunt Edna?"

Aunt Edna thought about that. She'd tried to think about it before, but there were so many things to think about that she'd ended up not thinking about it at all. But now she had to. "Well, she could sleep in my brother, Thomas's, room which would be nice because Thomas was her great grandfather." She paused and appeared to be listening to someone or something, but no one else was speaking. She nodded suddenly and said, "But of course the bed in there is a bit narrow and high. And the fireplace needs cleaning."

"We can clean the fireplace for you," Gerald said, but Aunt Edna wasn't listening. She was thinking.

Aunt Edna thought with all of her face. Her eyes moved from side to side, her mouth smiled and frowned, her cheeks puffed in and out, her eyebrows twitched up and down and thinking-out-loud words tumbled out of her mouth in no particular order. "She could sleep in my parents' bedroom. The bed is bigger and the fireplace works. But it faces south and doesn't get a lot of light." She paused suddenly as if listening to something over her right shoulder, then continued quickly. "Then there is my grandparents' bedroom, which is even bigger and faces east. It gets the morning sun and is very shady in the afternoon, and it's next to my bedroom." She paused again as if listening to something over her left shoulder. "Or there is the first guest room, but there is a lot of furniture in there and it's hard to get to the beds." Another pause and this time she nodded as if agreeing with someone, although else was speaking. "Or there is the second guest room, but that has even more furniture in it and you have to climb over things to get to the beds." Her head turned from side to side, her eyes vibrated, her mouth smiled and frowned, her cheeks puffed in and out, her eyebrows twitched up and down. And suddenly the words stopped, she gasped loudly, her teeth flew out of her mouth and her hand came up to catch them and pop them back in.

Then she held her finger up. She had made a decision! Everyone gathered around and waited to hear where Isobel would sleep.

"Isobel shall have my grandparents' room. Morning sun, afternoon shade. The bed is big and quite beautiful. It's not too cluttered. And it overlooks the rose garden. Yes. She shall have that room."

"Right!" Gerald turned to his helpers. "We'll start there and move from room to room."

Someone said, "What size mattress, Gerald?"

Gerald made his way through the crowd in the passage, looked into Isobel's new room and said, "It's a double, by the look of it."

Aunt Edna said, "Why do you want to know that?"

"Because," Gerald replied, "we figured you hadn't had a new mattress out here for as long as any of us can remember, and your niece should have a nice new one."

"Oh, but I haven't ordered a new mattress. Won't I have to order one from the mattress shop?"

Gerald pointed through the window to a truck parked in front of the house. "See that?"

"Yes. It's the mattress shop truck."

"Well, we came prepared. There are mattresses of every size in that truck and it's been decided that every bed in your house shall have a fresh new mattress. Even your bed, Aunt Edna."

Everyone was looking at her, nodding and smiling.

"Well, that's a very nice thought. I'd better get my purse ..."

"No, no. It won't cost you anything. The mattress shop would have gone out of business twenty years ago if you hadn't been there to help out. In fact, you've helped all of us out at one time or another, Aunt Edna. And now it's our turn to help you. We've brought mattresses, curtains, bedding, some farm clothes for Isobel and a lot of other things that you might need. And we've brought food for a slap-up barbecue when we've finished. How does that sound?"

Aunt Edna was quite overcome. Her eyes misted up and so did her glasses. She couldn't see a thing. She put her hand over her heart and nodded her thanks to everyone standing in the fog before her.

Isobel's bedroom was soon transformed. The peeling wallpaper was stripped away and the walls painted pale pink, which everyone considered appropriate for an eleven year old girl. The furniture was moved around to make more space, the windows washed and hung with new curtains, and the fireplace cleaned out. The room positively gleamed. When Isobel's bedroom was done, they moved onto the other rooms.

Someone found the linen cupboard and declared that all the sheets and bedding were in good condition, but they smelled a little stale and should be washed before making up Isobel's bed. Before long the clothesline, which was strung between two gum trees out the back, was full of washed sheets and blankets drying in the sun.

Aunt Edna was thrilled with all the activity. She hadn't had so many people in the house since the day of her husband's funeral when she'd decided not to bury him, but to freeze him instead.

An old record player was found and an opera record put on. Aunt Edna grinned with delight. She liked opera and hummed along to the sound of Madam Butterfly. Everyone found something to do. Aunt Edna gave directions when asked and busied herself in the kitchen, cooking up batches of biscuits for morning tea in Barking Wood Stove and making sandwiches and cakes for lunch. And still the cleaning, polishing, washing, painting and rearranging continued.

After lunch, Aunt Edna made more cakes and biscuits for afternoon tea. Everyone jumped each time Barking Wood Stove WOOFED. Finally, Aunt Edna carried kindling and stumps out to the old barbeque under the pepper tree behind the house and lit the fire.

As the sun started to set, Gerald led her through the house. She oohed and aahed at how sparkling and new everything looked, how fresh it smelled, how uncluttered and organised it was, and how she probably wouldn't be able to find anything anymore, but she'd have fun trying. She saw a new fridge in the kitchen and a new washing machine and tumble dryer in the laundry. Her sagging kitchen shelves had been rearranged and the bathroom was gleaming. She was very pleased.

Then Gerald took her out to the barbecue where trestle tables had been set up and the salads, meats and desserts had been laid out along side stacks of buttered bread and bottles of tomato sauce. Soon, the air was filled with the scent of sizzling sausages and frying onions and insect repellent and fly spray. There were stubbies of beer and cans of soft drink in old baby baths full of ice. Someone started playing John Farnham songs on their mobile phone and everyone sang along. A noisy, jolly slap-up Australian barbecue.

Diggidydog hung around until someone threw him a sausage, then he flopped under the pepper tree and munched away. Grumblebumkin sat high up in the pepper tree, looking down on the crowd below with disdain. Everyone was glad he was up the tree, for they all knew his fearsome reputation.

Aunt Edna looked around at her kind and generous friends and thought, "Yes. Now Isobel can come."

CHAPTER 4

Diamonds in Underpants and A Crinoline Petticoat

Isobel left Sydney on the plane early in the morning. Mr Hamble, the lawyer, accompanied her. He was very stern and did not talk much. They landed in Adelaide where a limousine awaited to drive them to Hopperfield. They drove out of the city and through the Adelaide Hills. Then the countryside became dry and brown and flat. Isobel, who was already feeling sad, felt even sadder when she saw it. Sydney had been green and lush. She didn't like the bare brown paddocks and the occasional dusty little towns they passed through.

Finally, they came to a bigger, more impressive town with a river running through it and a sign saying, "Welcome to Hopperfield".

Isobel thought it was strange to see a town with her own name on it. They stopped in the main street and asked for directions to Hopperfield Station. People came out of their shops and houses at the sight of the long black car. They knew who was in it, for the arrival of Aunt Edna's niece was big news. They tried to peer in to see what Isobel looked like, but the windows were tinted and they couldn't see anything.

Isobel looked out at a sea of strange faces and wished she was back in school in Sydney. No one ever looked at her there. She may as well have been invisible at school which was better than being stared at here.

Someone gave the driver directions and they drove on until they came to big gates with "Hopperfield Station" in large iron letters above it. There was her name again. They drove along a dusty track between towering gum trees, the branches swaying and rustling gently above them in the hot summer breeze. They seemed to be whispering, "welcome, Isobel, welcome". And then she saw the house. It was bigger than she expected. It looked like one of those grand old houses on the North Shore in Sydney where she had lived with her Mum and Dad.

Mr Hamble looked approvingly at the house and said, "That's a good start."

As the limousine pulled up in front of the house, an old lady in a brown dress and tatty old boots came out onto the veranda. She was wearing a big apron spattered in white stuff and brown stuff and yellow stuff and green stuff, and she held a wooden spoon dripping with more green stuff. A fat old dog with grey around its muzzle waddled down the front steps and grinned toothlessly up at the car.

There was a rickety cane table and six rocking chairs lined up on the veranda. An old ginger tabby cat sat on one of the chairs. When the car stopped, it leapt up onto the old lady's shoulders and draped itself around her neck like a scarf. She patted the cat gently, removed it and put it back on the chair. Then she came down the steps.

Mr Hamble got out of the car, walked towards the old lady and extended his hand. "Mrs Toddleby?"

But the old lady ignored him, walked right past him and went straight to the car. She opened the back door and stuck her head in, almost touching Isobel's face.

"You're here! Oh, dear, I've got flour and cocoa powder on my glasses. Been making you a chocolate omelette and broccoli custard for tea. Just a minute." She took off her very thick glasses and wiped them on her very spattered apron. When she put them back on, they were smeared with brown and white. "Nope. Still can't see you."

Isobel grinned. The old lady was funny and she smelled of chocolate and vanilla. Isobel leaned forward, took the old lady's glasses and wiped them clean with a tissue from her pocket. When she put them back on the old lady, the first thing she saw was big blue eyes. Kind eyes. Pleased eyes. Excited eyes.

The old lady said, "There you are! What a pretty little girl you are. And you have blue eyes, like me!" Isobel and the old lady grinned at each other. "I'm your Aunt Edna."

"Hello, Aunt Edna." Isobel completely forgot about being sad for a moment.

Mr Hamble came up behind Aunt Edna. "Mrs Toddleby?"

"What?" Aunt Edna stood up straight and looked at Mr Hamble. "Mrs Who?"

"Mrs Toddleby. You are Mrs Toddleby, aren't you?"

"Am I?" She looked down at herself. "Oh, yes, so I am."

Mr Hamble looked a little uncertain. He extended his hand again to shake hers, but she gave him the dripping wooden spoon instead and turned back to Isobel. Then she reached into the car and gently helped Isobel out. "Welcome home, dear girl, welcome home."

Mr Hamble was looking at the wooden spoon with dismay. He put it carefully on the bonnet of the limousine. The driver looked at it with disgust.

Aunt Edna continued to ignore Mr Hamble. After all, he wasn't important and he was going to leave soon, so why bother? She led

Isobel up the stairs to the veranda. "Meet the family, dear. This is Diggidydog. Say hello to Isobel, Diggidy." Diggidydog licked Isobel's hand and wagged his tail so hard that he nearly fell over.

"And this is Grumblebumkin." Grumblebumkin lowered his eyelids, raised his hackles and prepared to spit at Isobel. Aunt Edna narrowed her eyes and hissed at Grumblebumkin, "Don't even think about it! This is Isobel Hopperfield, Thomas's great granddaughter and my niece. And she'll need protecting from werewolves, just like I do!" Grumblebumkin opened his eyes in surprise, lowered his hackles and, like Diggidydog, licked Isobel's hand. Then he rubbed himself around Isobel's ankles, as cats do, to let her know she was accepted.

"Werewolves?" Isobel asked.

"Oh, you don't need to worry about them, dear. Not with Grumbley around. Now, you might meet the rest of the family and you might not. It will depend on whether you can see them or not."

"Pardon?"

"Oh, dear, I'm not explaining myself very well, am I? Come inside, Isobel. I've made some lemonade for you from the lemons on the tree that your own great grandfather planted. How about that, hey?"

Mr Hamble was following Aunt Edna up the steps. "Mrs Toddleby. Mrs Toddleby!"

Aunt Edna turned to him. He was an empty, irritating little man. "What is it?"

"We need to talk ..."

"Why? Are there more papers to sign?"

"Just one. And we need to discuss Isobel's return to school in Sydney in February."

"Return to school? Goodness, we don't have to think about school just yet, do we? No one wants to think about school when it's the holidays. Plenty of time for that later. What do I need to sign?"

"Just this, formalising the handing of Isobel over to your care as her guardian." He handed Aunt Edna a piece of paper and a pen. She signed on the dotted line and handed the paper and pen back.

Aunt Edna looked down at Isobel. "Do you have much luggage, dear?"

"Just a suitcase, Aunt Edna."

Aunt Edna addressed Mr Hamble. "You can leave Isobel's suitcase on the veranda. I'll get it later. And you can write one of your letters to let me know about the school thingy. Thank you for bringing her here and goodbye." She turned her back on Mr Hamble and went inside with Isobel, slamming the front screen door in Mr Hamble's face.

Mr Hamble stood there for a moment. He wasn't used to being dismissed like this. But there was nothing more to be done, so he put Isobel's suitcase on the veranda, got back in the car and drove away with the dripping wooden spoon on the bonnet.

Inside, Aunt Edna stood in the passage and looked at Isobel with a grin so wide it nearly split her face in two. "My very own niece. Who would have thought? And you're so very, very pretty. Blonde hair and blue eyes. Why, I think you look like me when I was your age. Well, never mind. You can't have everything, can you? Now, what do you want to do first? Would you like something to eat or drink? Or we could have a look at your room. It's got a new mattress and everything. Or we could have a look at the garden ..."

Isobel was staring at Aunt Edna with an uncertain smile on her face. Something about Aunt Edna reminded her of her grandfather and her father, something in the blue eyes and the kind mouth. And the memory of her parents and the home in Sydney that she would never see again rushed at her. She felt her lip tremble and her eyes filled with tears.

Aunt Edna stopped talking and looked at Isobel with dismay. "Oh, my dear, what is it?" Then she tilted her head to one side as if listening to something. "Oh. I see. Of course. Your dear Mummy and Daddy died, didn't they? And you're sad. Well, of course, you would be."

Aunt Edna suddenly pulled Isobel into an embrace that almost smothered her. Aunt Edna's big boobs squashed against her face and a cocoa covered belly wrapped around her nose and mouth. She twisted her head to get a breath, but she didn't pull away. Aunt Edna was soft and warm and smelled lovely. And the past six months had been so lonely. No one had hugged her.

Aunt Edna stepped back, looked down and said, "We need something to cheer you up. Would you like some diamonds?"

Diamonds were the last thing Isobel was expecting to hear. "I don't know. I've never had diamonds before."

"What, never? Then it's time you started. Such cheerful things, diamonds."

Aunt Edna wiped away Isobel's tears with the corner of her spattered apron, took her by the hand and led her into one of the bedrooms. A big iron bedstead in the middle of the room was draped with a brightly patterned quilt. A large painting of a pretty young woman and a handsome young man in old fashioned clothes hung on the wall behind the bed. The woman wore an elaborate white wedding dress with a skirt so wide that the man had to stand a little distance away from her. She had a tiny waist and big blue eyes. A wedding veil was secured to the woman's blonde hair with a row of flowers and a magnificent necklace hung from her neck. The man was rather short, unremarkable and wore a black suit with a high collar and a top hat. Isobel was captivated by the painting.

"Who is that?" she asked.

Aunt Edna barely glanced up. "Oh, that's just me and Bert on our wedding day. Such a lovely day it was. Everyone in the district was here. Weren't we a pretty pair?"

"The dress is awesome. And the necklace."

"Oh, you like the necklace? You can have it. If I can find it. Now, where did I see it last?"

Aunt Edna looked around the room, then went to a tall chest of drawers and started opening one drawer after another. She muttered to herself as she rooted around in the drawers, then began to throw things over her shoulder. Big lady underpants and nighties and linen handkerchiefs and worn petticoats and lots of brown socks. As each garment hit the floor, Isobel heard a clunk. She touched one of the rolled up socks with her foot and felt something hard inside. She picked the sock up and emptied the contents into her hand. It was a bracelet, a very sparkly bracelet with several rows of glittering gemstones set in gold. "Are these diamonds, Aunt Edna?"

Aunt Edna looked up briefly. "Of course, dear. I only have diamonds. So many diamonds. Such a nuisance to look after. I keep them wrapped in my underwear so they don't get dusty. Where oh where is that necklace?" She turned back to the task of finding the necklace and more articles of clothing hit the floor.

Isobel began to empty all of the diamonds out of Aunt Edna's underwear into a pile on the floor. She looked down to see rings, brooches, necklaces, bracelets and tiaras piled up at her feet. She loved how they sparkled and glittered.

Aunt Edna suddenly cried, "Here it is!" She untangled something from some old grey underpants and held it up victoriously. "My wedding necklace! My brother sent it to me from Africa. Along with all the other diamonds." She plonked it in Isobel's hand.

It was a large heavy necklace with two rows of big sparkling diamonds. Isobel spread it out with both hands and looked up at the painting again. "Can I try it on?"

"Of course, my dear. Do you want to try it on with the dress and veil?"

"Do you still have them?"

"Of course I do. I keep everything. Never know when it might come in handy."

Suddenly, Aunt Edna threw herself on the floor and slithered under the bed. "It's in a box here...somewhere...here it is." She pulled a big, flat box from under the bed and put it on top of the quilt. When she lifted the lid, Isobel saw only tissue paper at first. Then Aunt Edna peeled the paper away and pulled out the biggest dress Isobel had ever seen. It was snowy white with layers of lace and frills. "Hmm, we'll need the crinoline. That's in the cedar wardrobe," and she went to one of the wardrobes lined up against one wall. She pulled something out and turned to Isobel. "Hold your arms up."

Isobel raised her arms obediently and Aunt Edna slipped something over her head. She looked down. "What is this? It looks like a bird cage."

Aunt Edna threw her head back and roared with laughter. "A bird cage! Hahahaha! That's what my Bert used to call it! It's a crinoline petticoat, my dear, all the rage in 1860 and one of the silliest things ever invented. You couldn't get through a doorway with this on. You had to lift it up and go through sideways."

"Oh. What did it do?"

"You'll see." Aunt Edna took the dress, gathered the skirt up in her hands and dropped it down over Isobel's head. She arranged the veil on Isobel's blonde hair, spent a moment straightening the folds of the skirt, placed the necklace around her neck and turned her towards a large mirror.

Isobel gasped. She looked like one of those wedding cakes that start small at the top and get bigger and bigger as it goes down. The bottom of the dress almost filled the room. And the necklace came down to her waist. She looked so funny and so silly that she began to giggle.

Aunt Edna smiled. She had cheered her niece up and she was pleased. "You can play dress-ups in this any time you like, dear. I've got a lot of things you can play dress-ups in."

"Oh, Aunt Edna, this is like the most awesome thing ever!"

"Good. Now, how about we look at your room and see if it's up to scratch?"

"Alright."

"Better take this off first or you won't be able to get out of the room," and the wedding dress and crinoline came off to be tossed onto the bed. But the necklace stayed on.

Aunt Edna led Isobel into the room next door. Isobel stood in the middle of the room and turned slowly. "Is all this for me?"

"All of this is for you, my dear."

"Wow! It's so big and so pretty."

"So you like it?"

"It's like - wow!"

"I suppose that means you like it. Good."

"My room at home was small and I sleep in a dormitory at school."

"A dormitory? Oh, I don't like the idea of that. All that farting and snoring going on in the same room. I like a room to myself when I fart."

Isobel giggled. "You are funny, Aunt Edna."

"I've been told that before. Now, would you like something to eat?"

"I've already had something on the plane and it isn't lunch time yet..."

"Does that matter? I eat whenever I feel like it. Sometimes it's at six in the morning, sometimes it's at three in the afternoon, sometimes it's at midnight. So, are you hungry?"

"Suppose so."

"Come on, then, I'll introduce you to Barking Wood Stove."

"Barking Wood Stove?"

"Yes, dear. He keeps me from burning the house down, lovely old thing that he is. He's been keeping your omelette warm."

"Omelette?"

"Yes, you know. With eggs and melted chocolate and sardines and pepper and vanilla. Come on."

Aunt Edna bustled out of the bedroom and down the passage into the kitchen. Isobel hurried after her. "Should I get my suitcase?"

Aunt Edna called back over her shoulder, "Oh, don't bother. Diggidydog will get it." She suddenly yelled back down the passage towards the front door in a booming voice, "Diggidy! Suitcase! Isobel's room!"

As Aunt Edna disappeared into the kitchen, Isobel heard the squeak of the front screen door. She turned to see Diggidydog prising the door open with one paw. The handle of the suitcase was clamped firmly between his toothless gums. He opened the door just enough to get himself through, walked slowly up the passage with his legs spread so that he wouldn't trip over the suitcase, dropped it onto the floor of Isobel's room and came back into the passage. He turned to Isobel, gave her his huge toothless grin and went back outside to resume his nap.

Isobel chuckled. She liked Diggidydog. This was a fun place.

She hurried up the passage to the kitchen. She had completely forgotten to feel sad.

CHAPTER 5

Brown Omelette and Green Custard

The kitchen was hot and smelled of so many delicious things that Isobel stood for a moment and just sniffed. Aunt Edna was bent over a huge old blackened wood stove with two big ovens and six hotplates. She was looking at a frypan on one of the glowing red hotplates. She pointed a finger at it and said, "You can finish now." The hotplate glowed a little more, there was the sound of a large dog barking, followed by a wheezy cough as a puff of smoke shot out and the glow stopped.

Aunt Edna lifted the frypan and turned to Isobel with a smile. "There, now, done to perfection." She looked at the big table. "Too hot in here, dear. We'll eat outside." Aunt Edna pointed towards the back door. "Much nicer out there. We'll need a couple of plates - over there in that cupboard," she pointed with the frypan to a cupboard, "and knives and forks - over there in that drawer," she pointed to a drawer with her other hand, "and bring another chair out. The little one over by the wall will do." Then she picked up a jug from the table with her free hand and was out the back door.

Isobel looked around her in astonishment. Was she supposed to get all those things? Then she heard Aunt Edna call out from the back veranda, "Oh, and introduce yourself to Barking Wood Stove! I've already told him about you!"

Isobel was confused. How do you introduce yourself to a stove? Then the wood stove glowed a little and made a humming noise. It seemed friendly enough. She moved toward it. It glowed some more. She went up to it and said, as if it was the most natural thing in the world, "Hello, Barking Wood Stove. I'm Isobel." She heard a sizzle and a sigh. Two of the back hotplates glowed and half of the front middle hotplate glowed. It looked just like a smiley face. Isobel grinned.

Then she heard Aunt Edna call out again. "Plates, dear! Knives! Forks! Chair!"

Isobel hurried to get the items and joined Aunt Edna on the back veranda. It was certainly cooler out there, with the branches of the big pepper tree swaying gently above them in the breeze. As Aunt Edna set the little table, Isobel looked around.

Aunt Edna saw Isobel looking around. She pointed to the outbuildings. "That's the old stables over there - we used to have a lot of horses once - and that's the equipment shed over there and those big sheds behind them are the old shearing sheds. The horse yards and the sheep pens are behind them. And that," she said, pointing towards the hill, "is the Lightning Rock."

Isobel looked up toward the top of the hill and saw something glint in the sunlight. "What's that black shiny thing at the top?"

"Why, the Rock, of course. We'll go there after we've eaten. The waterhole is halfway up and it's a good day for a swim. Now, sit down and we'll have our snack."

Isobel sat down. Aunt Edna cut the brown omelette in half in the frypan and tipped Isobel's half onto her plate. Then she took the jug and poured something green and gooey all over it. Isobel gasped. It looked revolting. "What is that?"

"Broccoli custard, of course. What else would it be?"

Aunt Edna sat down and started to eat. Isobel picked up the knife and fork and looked down reluctantly. Aunt Edna glanced at her with surprise. "Not hungry after all, dear?"

"No. Well, yes. It's just that ..."

Aunt Edna suddenly looked over her shoulder, listened, and turned back. "Oh, you haven't had chocolate and sardine omelette with broccoli custard before?"

"No..."

"Just try a little bit, dear. If you don't like it, you don't have to eat it. That's the rule in this house. If you don't like something, you don't have to eat it, do it or have it. I certainly don't."

Isobel put a little of the green and brown on her fork, sniffed it and took a bite. There was a sudden explosion of delightful deliciousness inside her mouth. All those lovely things she smelled in the kitchen were in that tiny mouthful of food. She could taste chocolate, sardines, pepper and vanilla, as Aunt Edna had said, but there was also the taste of peaches and liquorice and biscuits cooking and steak barbecuing and onions frying and cinnamon and nutmeg and stewed apples and mint and lemon sherbet and watermelon and toffee and coconut curry and tomato sauce and rhubarb crumble and fresh bread and raspberry jam. It was miraculous!

Suddenly, she was very hungry indeed. She gobbled up the rest.

Aunt Edna finished, put down her knife and fork, patted her big tummy and let out a loud burp. Isobel giggled. Aunt Edna looked at her. "Well, go on," she said.

"Go on what?"

"Show your appreciation."

"How?"

Aunt Edna grinned her toothy grin, puffed out her wobbly chest, pulled her chin back into her wrinkled neck and let out a burp that resonated loudly around them. It was a long bubbly burp and when she was finished, she sighed with pleasure and patted her tummy again. "Now your turn, dear."

Isobel had been taught that burping was rude, so she was a bit shocked. But she gave it a try anyway. She rubbed her tummy, puffed out her skinny chest, tucked her chin in and burped. It was only a little one, but Aunt Edna was delighted.

"Not bad for a start. You'll get better at it. Practice makes perfect."

Isobel got up and started to collect the plates and cutlery.

Aunt Edna looked surprised. "What are you doing, dear?"

"Cleaning up. We always have to clean up our own plates at school."

"Oh, my, you don't need to do that here. Grumblebumkin will clean them." Aunt Edna looked up into the pepper tree. Isobel saw the cat sitting there on a low branch, watching them with superior eyes. "OK, Grumbley, you can come down now."

Grumblebumkin leapt elegantly from the branch onto the table, rubbed softly against Isobel's hand, then pushed it out of the way and proceeded to lick the plates clean.

Aunt Edna said, "We'll leave him to it. I think a swim is in order, don't you, dear?"

"That would be nice. We have a pool at school. I got my bronze medal last year."

"Bronze medal? Is that something good?"

"It's for swimming well."

"Oh. I don't swim well. I just dunk and splash. Fancy a bit of dunking and splashing?"

"Sure. I'll go get my swimmers."

"Swimmers?" Aunt Edna looked around. "Are there more of you?"

"My bathing suit."

"Ohhhh. Bathers. You won't need that. Much nicer to go in with your clothes on and let them dry on the way back. Very cooling." Aunt Edna looked at Isobel's pretty summer dress and sparkly sandals. "But they will never do, dear. Fine for the city, but not for the farm. Come on, my friends from town brought you some farm clothes. Let's go see what they got for you." She jumped up and went inside. Isobel hurried after her.

In Isobel's room, Aunt Edna went to a large chest of drawers next to the bed. "Now, let's see, I'm sure they were all put in here somewhere." She opened drawer after drawer and threw things over her shoulders at Isobel, just as she had done in the other bedroom. Isobel ducked, expecting more diamonds, but they were only clothes this time. "See if this fits ... try this on ... these thongs might do ...

these shorts look about right ... this t-shirt looks nice and light ... this hat should look good ... these shorts are much nicer ... brown, you see, doesn't show the dirt ... here are some more sandals ... oh, so much stuff here..."

Aunt Edna turned to see how Isobel was doing. She was almost buried under the clothes thrown at her. Isobel pulled the clothes off her and inspected them. These were definitely not the sort of clothes she was used to. Aunt Edna saw her indecision and decided for her. "That t-shirt. Those shorts. This hat. And these thongs. I'll wait out the back for you. And best leave the necklace here. Diamonds are so easy to lose. Lost lots of them around the farm when I was younger."

Isobel dressed quickly and joined Aunt Edna out on the back veranda where Grumblebumkin was licking the last of the plates clean. "You look just right, dear," Aunt Edna said with an approving nod at the brown shorts, brown t-shirt, brown thongs and big straw hat. Then she took her old hat from the hook on the back veranda, jammed it on her head and strode off towards the hill. Isobel made sure her own hat was on properly and rushed after her. Aunt Edna didn't give you much time to think about anything.

As they went past the old stables, Isobel glanced in. She could see they were deserted and was surprised at how big the building was. "How many horses did you have, Aunt Edna?"

Aunt Edna stopped and turned around. "How many? Hmm, let me think. When I was a little girl, we had a lot. No tractors or cars in those days. Well, we had the Clydesdales, about fifteen of those. The bush brumbies - my father used to train them here and sell them to other farmers. Then there were the ponies for me and Thomas and the horses for the carriages. And of course, we had the race horses, Arabians mostly. Grandpa was a great horse breeder. Must have had over fifty horses here, sometimes a hundred and fifty. Why, dear, do you like horses?"

"Yes. I have riding lessons twice a week at school."

"Really? What sort of riding?"

"Jumping. Cross country. A bit of dressage."

"Hmm. Would you like a horse of your own then?"

"Oh, yes. I always wanted my own horse."

"Then you shall have one. We'll see to it tomorrow. But ..."

"But?"

"Well, dear, when we had horses, we had lots of stable hands. They used to muck out the stalls and look after the horses. I'll have to find someone to do that."

"I can do that. We had to do that at school."

"Sounds like a very practical school. It would be nice to have a horse back in the stables. And I just might get a horse of my own, too. I miss old Sir Galahad. Although The Great Smoking Beastie might get a bit jealous. Hhmm, never mind, I'll talk to him and explain. We can go riding together. Would you like that?"

"Sure."

"I could take you all over the farm and show you everything ... well, maybe not all over it. We'll have to give the Zombie Paddock a wide berth ..."

"Zombie Paddock?"

But Aunt Edna was already pushing on and Isobel rushed to keep up with her.

They entered the track that wound up the hill. It was instantly cooler here under the ancient gum trees and so quiet that Isobel could hear their footsteps softly crunching beneath them. The air smelled of eucalyptus and sweet soil. Isobel thought it was magical with the dappled light and scented air.

After a few minutes of climbing, Isobel could smell water. Then she heard it bubbling out of the ground ahead of her. They came around a bend in the track and there was the waterhole, tranquil and shady under the canopy of gum trees. It was about the size of a big swimming pool, but it was roundish rather than square. Ferns grew around the edges and a small waterfall cascaded into it at one end.

Aunt Edna suddenly shrieked with delight, took a running leap towards the waterhole, wrapped her arms around her knees and landed with a splash in the water, boots and all. For a second, all Isobel could see was her hat sitting on top of the water, then Aunt Edna's wet face appeared with that toothy grin that Isobel liked so much and water dripping from her chin. She shook the water from her glasses, straightened them on her nose, tossed the hat into the ferns at the edge of the waterhole and cried out, "Come on, dear! It's lovely! And it's not too deep. I can stand up, see?" She stood up and the water came to her chest.

It looked irresistible. Isobel put her hat on the ground, kicked off her thongs and took a flying leap into the water. It was brilliant! As she went under, she opened her eyes and there in front of her was a big fish staring right at her. She splashed to the surface. "There's a fish in here!"

"Oh, there are lots of fish in the waterhole. We'll stop by on the way back and collect a couple for later. Nothing like a bit of fresh fish and some crisp hot chips for tea, is there?"

Isobel saw something poking out of the water near the waterfall. "What's that, Aunt Edna?"

Aunt Edna glanced in the direction Isobel was pointing. "Oh, that's just the pipe that carries the water down to the house and the outbuildings. My Pa put that in during the Big Drought. The waterhole never runs dry, you see, so we have pure spring water in abundance. Marvellous for hot baths and growing broccoli. Now, let's just float for awhile, hey?"

Aunt Edna let her body rise to the surface and she floated on her back, her wet boots sticking up and her arms spread out beside her. She looked up through her thick wet glasses and sighed.

Isobel copied her. The water around them became as still as glass and Isobel felt the silence of the bush seep into her mind. It was so peaceful, and she hadn't felt peaceful since she'd heard about her parents. They floated until their heads touched and stared up through the trees.

CHAPTER 6

A Secret Shared and Rocks in a Coffin

Then Aunt Edna said, ever so quietly, "Can you keep a secret, dear?"

"Sure."

"Then perhaps this is a good time to tell you a story."

"What sort of story?"

"A story about the Lightning Rock."

"Alright."

"But it's a story that only Hopperfields should know about and you are a Hopperfield."

"I won't tell. Promise."

"Good girl. Well, it all started on a day just like this. I was about your age and I met Murungul right here at the waterhole."

"Who's Murungul?"

"He was an old Aboriginal man. Very, very old. So old, he was transparent."

"How can a person be transparent?"

"When they are ready to die, they start to fade away."

"You mean ... like you can see through them?"

"Oh yes. That's how you know when it's their right time to die. When it's not their right time, they stay solid. Like the zombies."

"Zombies?"

"Well, of course. Poor dears. They have to hang around being undead until it's their time and they can finally go to the Other Side. Terribly boring for them."

"But aren't zombies scary?"

"Oh goodness no. I have a whole paddock full of them."

"A whole paddock?" Isobel looked around her with alarm.

"Yes, but they're all underground at present, so they won't bother you. They don't like the heat, you see. Much cooler underground. They come out at night sometimes, but only when something disturbs them. Don't keep interrupting me, dear. I haven't finished my story yet."

"Oh. Sorry Aunt Edna." Isobel relaxed again and looked up through the trees.

"Now, where was I? Oh yes. I was at the waterhole with Murungul. My brother Thomas was with me. Thomas was two years older than me. We were floating in the waterhole, just like we are now, and Thomas looked over and there was Murungul standing in the middle of the track. Thomas and I got out of the water and I asked Murungul what he was doing here."

"What did he say?"

"Well, dear, he told us that this was his country, his birthplace and he'd swum in this waterhole like we were doing when he was a little boy. When he grew up, he went walkabout and lived somewhere else. Now, he was the last one of his family left. He said that he'd come back to the spirit place on top of the hill to join his family in corroboree. That's an Aboriginal ceremonial dance. I asked him how he was going to do that if all his family were dead. He told me there was a big storm coming and when the three-pronged blue lightning came, he would see his family on the big black rock at the top of the hill and he would join them there as a spirit."

"Oh wow."

"Thomas thought he was a bit mad because there were no clouds in the sky, no sign of a storm coming and dancing spirits seemed rather silly. So he went home because it was almost time for tea. But I stayed with Murungul. He looked very tired, poor dear, so I put my arm around him and helped him the rest of the way to the top of the hill. Then I sat down with Murungul next to the black rock. He said, 'I am very weak, Little Missus. You got to help me call up the storm.' I said, 'How do I do that?' He said, 'You just think about storms. Like this,' and he closed his eyes and concentrated. So I did the same. I thought about thunder and lightning and rain. Then quick as a flash, black clouds formed above us, the wind blew through the trees and the storm was there. Just like that. Like magic. I asked Murungul what would happen next. He said, 'Were you born here, Little Missus?' I said, 'Yes, and my brother, too.' He said, 'I tell you the secret of the Lightning Rock. It is a secret only for people born on this land, like you, and for all your descendants.' Which means you, Isobel.'"

"Awesome."

"He said to me, 'When it is your time to die, you must come up here and call up a storm. When the blue lightning splits into three and hits the big black rock, you sing for your family spirits to come and when you see them dancing corroboree, you dance with them. The blue lightning will come again all around you and make you one of the spirits. But first you got to make a trade, you got to leave something for the country.' Then he looked at me with his old brown eyes and said, 'I bring seeds of the trees that were here when I was a boy, before the whitefella cleared it for the farms.' He showed me a small pouch of seeds that he wore tied around his neck. He said, 'I bring them to leave for the country, but now I think I leave something better than seeds. I think I leave you for this country, Little Missus. You born here, like old Murungul, so you part of this country. You can be my trade with the Lightning Rock.' I didn't know what he meant."

Isobel thought Murungul was very mysterious and tried to imagine what he might have looked like. "Did he say anything else?"

"I asked him what I was supposed to do. He handed me his pouch of seeds and said, 'Just you listen to this country. When you hear it speak, you know what to do.' He got up and went towards the rock. I was going to follow him, but he said, 'No, Little Missus, you got to stay off the rock. This not your time to join your family spirits. You make backward magic if you go on the rock before your time.' So I stood back from the rock and watched. And then it happened."

"What happened?"

"The wind was howling and the trees were blowing around and I thought it was the wildest storm I'd ever seen. Scary and exciting all at once. Then a three-pronged bolt of blue lightning hit the rock and Murungul started singing a song in his own language. He had two sticks he beat together and as he sang, I saw Murungul's family appear in front of me like ghosts and they were dancing corroboree. I heard their didgeridoos and I saw their painted faces. They made a space for Murungul in the centre of their dance and he walked onto the rock and joined them. The three-pronged blue lightning hit the rock again and Murungul stepped out of his old body and became a spirit man. The old body turned to dust in front of me and Murungul joined his family in the corroboree. He turned to me, smiled and waved. Then a single bolt of white lightning struck the centre of the rock and they were all gone. Just like that."

"Wow! Did that really happen?"

"It certainly did, my dear."

"What did you do then?"

"Well, I was so surprised, I just sat down. The clouds and the wind disappeared as quickly as they had come. A few moments later, Dad and Thomas turned up on their horses. They had seen the storm and the lightning and they were worried about me. I tried to tell them what had happened, but of course they didn't believe me. Dad put me on the back of his horse and as we rode away, I looked back, and there, in the middle of the rock was a perfect little pile of dust that had once been Murungul. Just sitting there in the stillness. And I knew it had been real."

"That's like the best story ever!" Isobel stood up and squeezed the water out of her hair. "Did you ever see another storm like that again?"

Aunt Edna stood up and shook the water from her hair the way a dog shakes when it's wet. Her teeth shot out of her mouth and she caught them just before they hit the water. She popped them back in and peered at Isobel through her wet glasses. "Yes, but not for a long time. I grew up and married my Bert and we stayed on the farm, but I didn't see the blue lightning or go onto the black rock again until I was old. As old as I am now. Which was a long time ago."

"I don't understand."

Aunt Edna sighed deeply. "Such a sad story, dear. My Bert died suddenly while he was out riding. That was more than a hundred years ago, but it's seems like yesterday to me."

"What happened to him?"

"His poor old heart just stopped. It was a terrible shock and I hadn't been able to say goodbye. That's very sad, isn't it, dear, when you can't say goodbye?"

Isobel thought about her Mum and Dad who had died so far away. She hadn't been able to say goodbye to them, not even at the airport. She'd been at boarding school the day they had flown to England. "Yes, it's very sad."

"So Bert was dead and we put him in a coffin on the dining room table and people came from all over the district to pay their respects. The undertakers..."

"What's that?"

"Undertakers? They bury dead people, dear. They came the day before the funeral and put the lid on the coffin and left me here, all alone, to watch over him until the next morning. I sat by his coffin and cried and cried, and then I remembered Murungul and the Lightning Rock. I thought perhaps if I took Bert up there and called up a storm, maybe I would see his spirit one last time and tell him I loved him and say goodbye. So I took him out of the coffin..."

"By yourself?"

"Oh, he was such a skinny little man, dear, it was no effort at all. Anyway, I took him out of the coffin and put him in my mother's old wheelchair - had to use one of my father's old belts to tie him in - and pushed him up here. He was in the blue striped pyjamas that he liked so much and I thought he looked very nice. We got to the top and I called up a storm, just as I had done all those years ago with Murungul. It was almost daylight when the wind came up and the clouds gathered above us. I pushed Bert onto the Lightning Rock and waited. And then the lightning started. Just a single bolt at first, then a couple of double bolts, and then, finally, a three-pronged blue bolt."

Aunt Edna paused with a little frown on her face.

"What's wrong, Aunt Edna?"

"Well, dear, I don't think I was meant to be on the Lightning Rock with my Bert. I think I should have been watching from the side, like Murungul had told me to."

"Why? What happened?"

"I was in the middle of the rock with Bert when the bolt of blue lightning came. Goodness, it made me jump! It hit the rock all around me. Then I remembered how Murungul had called to his family, so I called out Bert's name. I said, 'Bert, dearest, come to me so that we may talk, for I have things to tell you.' At first, nothing happened. I called again, and I saw spirit figures gathering around me. But they weren't Aborigines doing corroboree. They were ghosts in long nightdresses and nightshirts and they looked familiar. They were peering at me with surprised looks on their faces. One of them was my own dear Bert, standing there in his blue striped pyjamas. And then I saw that I had turned blue and there were blue sparks coming out of my fingertips. I tingled all over and I felt all nervous and jumpy. Diggidydog and Grumblebumkin had followed me onto the rock and they were blue and sparkly as well. We were bouncing all over the rock and the spirits were watching us like we were mad. And then a bolt of white lightning struck the rock and the storm stopped and..."

Isobel held her breath.

"...and I looked around me and saw the spirits of my dear Bert, my darling Ma and Pa and my old Granny and Grandpa standing around me. And they were not pleased."

"They weren't? Why not?"

"Bert said to me, 'What have you done, Edna?' I said, 'I just wanted to see you one last time.' He said, 'You have called us back from the Other Side and now we can't leave.' I said, 'Why not?' He said, 'Because you didn't make a trade with the Lightning Rock and so there was no second bolt of blue lightning.' I said, 'It'll come soon, won't it?' He said, 'Not now. The white lightning closed the door to the Other Side.' I said, 'What is the Other Side?' He said, 'It's where we all were. Where all the dead ones go. It was nice there. Quiet and restful. And now we can't go back. You made backward magic, Edna and it can't be undone.' I said, 'Oh.'"

"Just Oh?"

"Just Oh. Well, what can you say at such a time?"

Isobel thought Aunt Edna had a point there. "And then what happened?"

"Ma said, 'It wasn't your time, Edna. When the blue lightning struck, it made you an Eternal instead of a spirit. You are an Eternal now.' I said, 'What is that?' She said, 'It means you will never get older, never get tired, never get sick and never die.'"

"Awesome."

"My sentiments exactly."

"So you brought back a bunch of ghosts and you became a..."

"An Eternal." Aunt Edna rolled her eyes. "Such a bore, I know, but there it is."

Isobel did not think it was a bore at all. "Then what did you do?"

"What could I do? I said, 'Well, you'd better come down to the house for a cup of tea.' And they did."

"A cup of tea? Can ghosts do that?"

"Oh, yes, but it makes a terrible mess. Goes straight through them, you see. Leaves puddles all over the chairs."

Isobel tried to imagine ghosts sipping tea. Then she remembered Bert. "What happened to dead Bert in the wheelchair? Did he turn to dust like Murungul?"

"No. That only happens when someone is fading and is ready to pass over to the other side. My Bert had already passed. And now his ghost was back and I was left with dead Bert in the wheelchair as well."

"Did you put him back in the coffin?"

Aunt Edna pouted a little. "I know I should have, but it was so nice having him there. So I put him in the new freezer on the back veranda instead."

Isobel gasped. "In the freezer?"

"Yes, dear. It was brand new and shiny back then. I wheeled him into the back of the freezer and made a false wall, just in case anyone else should ever go in there. They might not understand."

"What about the under...under..."

"The undertakers?"

"Yes. Didn't they know the coffin was empty?"

"I put some big rocks in the coffin and off we went to the funeral. It was nice knowing he wasn't in that box. I didn't cry at all. When everyone had gone home, I went out to the freezer with a glass of lemonade and told Frozen Bert all about the funeral. And then I cooked dinner for Ghost Bert and the family. It was nice." Aunt Edna smiled to herself. It had indeed been a nice dinner.

Isobel stared at Aunt Edna with wide eyes. "Is he still there? In the freezer?"

"Oh, yes. Frozen is frozen, isn't it? Lasts a long time."

Aunt Edna tilted her head to one side and listened to something. Isobel suddenly understood what she was doing. "Are they talking to you now, Aunt Edna? The ghosts?"

"Hmm? Talking? Oh yes. Pa said it's getting late and little girls shouldn't be out after dark, which is nonsense of course. I was always roaming around the farm at night when I was your age. Marvellous place to roam around. All sorts of critters and creatures about at night. Well, that's enough of this. Let's go up to the Lightning Rock and call up a storm." And Aunt Edna was off. She leapt onto the bank, jammed her hat back on her head and strode up the track, her clothes dripping a string of puddles as she went and her wet boots squeaking with each stride. She called out behind her, "Come on, dear, keep up!"

Isobel scrambled onto the bank, grabbed her thongs and hat and ran after Aunt Edna.

CHAPTER 7

The Lightning Rock Trade and Calling Up a Storm

Isobel was puffing when they got to the top of the hill. Before them was a big, shiny, flat black rock, about as big as a football field. It gleamed and shimmered under the late afternoon sun. Isobel put her hand on the rock, expecting it to be hot, but it was icy cold. Very strange indeed.

Aunt Edna walked around the edge of the rock until she came to a couple of big boulders. She sat down on one of them and patted the other one. "Come over here, dear. It's best to be sitting when you call up a storm."

Isobel sat next to Aunt Edna and looked around. She could see the surrounding countryside for miles in every direction. The house below them looked very small. Apart from the house and the farm buildings, all she could see were flat paddocks. Some were brown, but some were green with trees and scrub and seemed to spread out all the way to the horizon. The green paddocks closest to the Lightning Rock had tall trees, but the trees in the distance were smaller. She pointed to the green paddocks. "Why do some of the paddocks have trees and others don't?"

Aunt Edna peered in the direction Isobel was pointing. "That's the trade. That's what the country told me to do."

"Oh, like Murungul said?"

"That's right."

"What exactly was the trade?"

"It was to plant trees and restore the land."

"How did the country tell you?"

"Well, it was after Bert's funeral which wasn't his funeral at all, of course. It was a funeral for rocks. Anyway, everyone had gone home, I was here alone and there was a lovely silvery moon that night. I came outside to have a look at it and I heard a sort of hum. It seemed to be coming from behind the shearing sheds. I followed the noise, but it kept moving away. I followed it into the paddock behind the Lightning Rock and the hum stopped. It was winter and there was only stubble in the paddock. I was about to go back to the house when I felt a tremor under my feet."

"Like an earthquake?"

"Yes, but only a little earthquake. And then the ground around me started to crack and open up..."

"Gosh."

"...and something came out of the cracks. I knelt down to see what it was and there were plants, little plants coming up through the soil. Well, I thought I must be dreaming, but of course, I don't sleep. Eternals don't get tired and we never sleep. So I couldn't be dreaming, could I?"

"No, I guess not."

"The plants kept coming up all around me and they grew so fast, next thing I know I was standing in a forest. Just like that. Stubble one minute, a forest the next, with birds and animals and insects. It was lovely. Then it faded away as quickly as it had come and the paddock was bare again. I heard a sigh all around me, like the country was sad. I understood then what I had to do. I went inside and rummaged around in my old bedroom and found that pouch of seeds that Murungul had given me. I'd kept them all those years. I planted them where I had felt the earth tremor, but of course, they didn't grow straight away. The paddock looked no different. So first thing the next morning, I saddled my horse and rode into town. There was a plant nursery behind the old bakery back then. I bought some little trees and planted them in the paddock behind the Lightning Rock. Over the years I learned how to collect seeds and grow them myself and I've been planting them ever since. Thousands of the dear little things. I turned the old equipment shed into a nursery of sorts and I spend many nights in there planting seeds and potting up seedlings."

"Wow, that's so cool. That's being environmental. How many acres have you planted?"

"I've been planting about a hundred acres a year."

"That's a lot."

"The farm is 50,000 acres. Still a lot of bare paddocks to plant up yet."

"That's going to take you a long time, Aunt Edna."

"Well, dear, if one is going to be an Eternal, one should have something to do. Right?"

Isobel thought about that. "Guess so." She looked up at the clear blue summer sky. "I can't see any storm."

"It's usually like this to begin with. We have to call it up. Just think storm."

"How do you think storm?"

"Think lightning and thunder and clouds and wind."

"OK." Isobel closed her eyes and tried to imagine a storm. Then something occurred to her and she opened her eyes. "Can I call up Mum and Dad if I see the blue lightning?"

Aunt Edna put her hand over Isobel's hand and said kindly, "I'm afraid not, Isobel. It only works for people who die here. Sorry, dear."

Isobel sighed. "That's OK. I kinda thought it wouldn't work."

Isobel closed her eyes and concentrated again. She felt a breeze caress her cheek and looked up. There was a tiny cloud above her, just a whisper of white fluff in the sky. It quickly grew and darkened and then it began to swirl. Within minutes, it was looming over the Lightning Rock and a howling wind whipped Isobel's hair across her face. She had to hang onto the boulder for fear of being blown away.

The first bolt of white lightning nearly made Isobel jump out of her skin. It hit the rock, exploding white sparks all around her. She glanced at Aunt Edna who'd seen all this before and saw that she was sitting calmly with her hands folded in her lap. Isobel thought that if Aunt Edna wasn't scared, then she wouldn't be either.

The second bolt was double-pronged and had a faint pink tinge to it. Isobel felt her hair beginning to stand on end. She knew about static electricity from the school science lab when she'd had to put her hand on a special globe with electricity going through it and her hair had stood on end. She looked at Aunt Edna again and started to laugh. Aunt Edna's hair was definitely standing on end, sticking straight out in every direction.

Aunt Edna grinned just as the third bolt struck. It was a big one, three pronged and brilliant blue. It hit the rock with an explosion and Aunt Edna's teeth shot out and flew into the air above them. She held out her hand, waited for the teeth to come back down, caught them and popped them back in.

Isobel felt a sudden surge of energy go through her, from the soles of her feet to the top of her head. Her fingers tingled and she held up her hands. They were blue! Blue sparks flew out of her fingertips. Aunt Edna held up her own blue sparking hands and touched Isobel's fingers. Energy pulsed through them both, so much energy that they simply had to get up and dance. The storm raged over them as they danced around and around the Lightning Rock, springing into the air like ballet dancers, flinging their arms around and moving to a rhythm that Isobel couldn't hear, but could feel in every part of her body. It was thrilling!

Then the next bolt of lightning struck, another three-pronged blue bolt, and suddenly everything stopped. The wind stopped, the noise stopped, the storm cloud shrivelled up and disappeared and they were standing on top of the hill watching a beautiful sunset on a perfectly still and quiet summer's evening.

Aunt Edna was delighted. She slapped her thigh and exclaimed, "That was a goody!"

Isobel couldn't agree more. She opened her mouth to say so, but Aunt Edna declared,

"Enough of this. Time to catch our dinner." And she was off at a trot.

Isobel ran down the track after her. She caught up at the waterhole just as Aunt Edna took her hat off and held it out over the water. A silvery fish jumped out of the water into the hat. Aunt Edna said, "Two for dinner tonight, thank you," and another fish jumped into the hat. Then she was off again and Isobel had to run all the way down to the house. She didn't think old ladies ran like that, but then, Aunt Edna was no ordinary old lady.

CHAPTER 8

Midnight on the Veranda and Ghostly Snacks

Isobel peeled and cut potatoes into chips while Aunt Edna scaled and cleaned the fish. A pot of oil was put on the stove to heat and Aunt Edna mixed bread crumbs and broccoli to make a stuffing for the fish. Barking Wood Stove cooked them perfectly. Isobel belched loudly to Aunt Edna's delight and then they washed the dishes. After dinner, Aunt Edna helped unpack Isobel's suitcase, showed her where everything was in the bathroom and said goodnight about 8.00pm.

    Isobel lay in her lovely new bed and looked at the silver moon through her bedroom window. She thought about Aunt Edna's silver moon all those years ago after Bert's funeral.

She thought about paddocks that hummed and forests that appeared out of nowhere and Aunt Edna planting thousands of little trees for a hundred years. Then she thought about the blue lightning and felt sad that it wouldn't work for her Mum and Dad. She didn't like feeling sad, but she often did at night when she was all alone in her bed.

She heard a thumping sound on the floor next to her bed. It was Diggidydog's long tail. He sat next to the bed, looking up at her with his big toothless grin, then licked her hand, lay down and closed his eyes. Something soft touched her cheek and she heard purring. Grumblebumkin rubbed his face against hers and curled up on the pillow. The sadness drained away. She was not alone. She drifted off to sleep with the thump-thump of Diggidydog's tail on the floor and Grumblebumkin purring softly in her ear.

Isobel wasn't sure what woke her. Diggidydog and Grumblebumkin hadn't moved. Then she smelled warm chocolate cake and heard Aunt Edna's footsteps down the passage. The front screen door squeaked open and shut with a soft thud. There was something going on.

Isobel got up and went into the passage. Diggidydog and Grumblebumkin woke up and followed her. The house was in darkness, but she could see the moonlit garden through the front screen door. She opened it slowly and looked out onto the veranda. Diggidydog and Grumblebumkin pushed past her quietly and sat on the front steps.

At first, she only saw Aunt Edna there in the moonlight, sitting on the rocking chair nearest to the door. There was chocolate cake and a big teapot on the small round table. Aunt Edna had a plate of cake on her lap and was sipping tea from a cup and saucer as her chair creaked to and fro.

Then Isobel saw that the other five chairs were rocking to and fro as well, even though there was no one on them. Suspended in space halfway up the moving chairs were five cups and saucers. As Isobel looked on, the cups lifted off the saucers and poured tea onto the chairs. All by themselves.

Isobel thought she must be dreaming. She closed her eyes and tried to feel asleep, but she only felt more awake. She blinked a couple of times. Then she felt a tingling in her fingertips and looked down to see blue sparks flying out of the end of each finger. When she looked up again, she saw not only Aunt Edna, but five old people sitting in the rocking chairs. Shimmering, glowing, transparent old people.

Two of them were old ladies wearing high-necked white embroidered nightdresses, which covered them down to the ankles so that only their slippers could be seen underneath. One of the ladies wore an old fashioned nightcap over her grey hair which hung in a long braid down her back, and she had a nose that was so pointy it looked like a bird beak. The other lady had snowy white hair in a neat bun at the back of her neck, a little snub nose and a face full of soft wrinkles.

The other three were old men. Two of them wore funny old nightshirts that buttoned down the front and came to their knees, their gnarled legs and feet sticking out underneath. One had white, wispy hair down to his shoulders and a long beard and moustache. Another was mostly bald with a ring of grey hair around the back of his head.

The third one was a skinny little man with thin grey hair and a bald patch on top of his head. He was wearing blue striped pyjamas.

Blue striped pyjamas. Isobel gasped. It had to be ghost Bert! Then the others must be…

Aunt Edna heard the gasp and looked up so suddenly that her teeth flew out of her mouth and, this time, it was Isobel who caught them before they hit the ground.

Aunt Edna took the teeth from Isobel, popped them back in and said, "You can see them, dear? The ghosts?"

Isobel nodded.

Aunt Edna looked very pleased. "Well, thank goodness for that. Makes life so much easier. I was dreading all the creeping around we'd have to do."

"But how…"

"Must have been the blue lightning. Changes things, you see. But don't worry, you aren't an Eternal. You have to be standing on the rock when the lightning strikes to become an Eternal. You weren't on the rock, but you must have got a touch of the lightning's magic." Aunt Edna grinned. "So, come and meet your family."

Isobel took an uncertain step forward.

"It's alright, dear, they won't bite. Ghosts can't, you know. They're teeth will go straight through you. Now, this is my mother and father - you can call them - oh what are they - your great-great-great grandparents? That's too many greats. Just call them Ma and Pa. And this is my old Granny and Grandpa. You can call them ... Granny and Grandpa."

The ghosts rose and floated towards Isobel, their transparent faces smiling and their eyes shining with pleasure. Or moonlight. Or just ghostliness. Isobel wasn't sure which. As they left their chairs, the cups and saucers fell to the ground, smashed into pieces and scattered china and tea all over the veranda.

Aunt Edna rolled her eyes and sighed. "Goodness, ghosts are messy creatures. It's a good thing I have plenty of spare cups and saucers. Remember that, Isobel - never use the good china with ghosts."

Isobel nodded. "OK."

She didn't know what to do next. How do you greet a ghost? Can you shake hands with a ghost? Can you kiss a ghost on the cheek? Do you say, "Yikes, you're a ghost!" or "Nice to see through you?" That didn't sound right and she didn't want to offend anyone, so she kept it simple and just said, "Hello."

The ghosts all began to talk at once in whispery voices. Ma, the one with the bun and little snub nose, gushed, "My dear child! So delighted to have you home!"

Granny, the one with the long braid and beak-like nose, exclaimed, "Oh my, you look just like Edna when she was a girl. Such a pretty little thing."

Pa, the bald one with a ring of hair around the back of his head, declared, "Good strong legs. A rider's legs. She'll do well with a horse of her own, Edna."

Grandpa, the one with the wispy white hair and beard, said agreeably, "Yes, a horse is a splendid idea."

Bert said kindly, "Welcome, child, welcome to Hopperfield Station. Come, you must have a cup of tea with us."

Isobel was overwhelmed and looked from ghost to ghost.

Aunt Edna interrupted. "I think a piece of cake and a cup of tea would be a nice start. Midnight snacks are always such fun. And it's not every day that a Mere Mortal sees you all, is it? In fact, it has never happened before. Fancy that." She suddenly raised her finger. "But first, I must get more cups and saucers." She ran inside and quickly returned with a tray of cups and saucers. She tossed them into the air and the ghosts caught them. Or almost caught them. The cups and saucers stopped in midair, but the ghosts' hands passed straight through them. The ghosts sat in their chairs and the cups and saucers took up their place in front of each chair.

Isobel said, "Awesome." She looked around and wondered where she should sit.

Aunt Edna shook her head. "Silly me. You should have your own chair. All of these are soggy with tea." She dashed around the side of the house and returned with another rocking chair. She lined it up with the others and Isobel sat down. Aunt Edna poured her a cup of tea and cut her a big slice of chocolate cake. Then she filled up the ghosts' cups and handed each one a piece of cake, which floated in the air next to the cups and saucers.

And there they all were, rocking to and fro in the moonlight, sipping tea and eating chocolate cake on a perfectly still moonlit night. Five shimmering ghosts, one Eternal and one Mere Mortal. Not to mention a toothless old Labrador and a bad tempered cat to clean up the puddles of tea and the chocolate cake crumbs later on.

Isobel watched pieces of cake break off in front of the ghosts, float into the ghostly mouths and drop right through them. It didn't seem to matter that it all ended up in a wet mess on the chairs, for each ghost chewed as if they had that cake inside their mouths and it was the most delicious thing in the world.

Grandpa said, "You make a good chocolate cake, Edna."

"Thank you, Grandpa."

Pa said, "We must find a horse for Isobel without delay."

Aunt Edna said, "Indeed. But it should be a pony for such a little girl. And if Isobel has a horse, so must I. A big one, like Sir Galahad. I miss galloping through the paddocks." She got up and went down the steps, then licked her finger and held it up. "There is no breeze, so it's a good night for you all to go horse hunting. You won't get blown around tonight."

Ma said, "Oh good. It's so tiresome when it's windy and we can't go outside. Now, let me see. The Hansons have a good stable. I'll go there first."

Granny said, "The Sullivans used to have some ponies. Haven't visited the Sullivans in a while. I'll look in on them."

Pa said, "Those new people who moved into the old Weston place had a horse float with them. I will pay them a visit. See if any horses came with the float."

Grandpa said, "That horse trainer who wants to retire to the coast. I'll cast an eye over his property."

Bert said, "The Miller children used to have horses. I'll go there."

Aunt Edna said, "Excellent! Well, off you go."

The ghosts floated off the veranda, all faced different directions and suddenly took off with a zoom. Isobel tried to see where they went, but they were gone before she could blink. She yawned.

Aunt Edna said sympathetically, "Mere Mortals need their sleep. Back to bed for you, dear."

"What if they find a horse for me?"

"I will wake you up, never fear." She took Isobel by the hand and led her inside. As she tucked Isobel back into bed, she said, "I think a special breakfast for you in the morning, being your first breakfast here."

Isobel realised it was still the same day that she had arrived. It was very strange because so much had happened that she felt she had been at Hopperfield Station a lot longer.

Aunt Edna continued, "Perhaps ginger biscuits with curry icing and a nice cheesy tuna, cherry and broccoli casserole. What do you think?"

"I usually have porridge."

"Porridge? That doesn't sound very imaginative, but I can make you some broccoli porridge if you like."

"I'd rather have chocolate cake. Why does everything here have broccoli in it, Aunt Edna?"

Aunt Edna looked at Isobel as if that was a silly question. "Because it is vampire season, of course. I'll go talk to Barking Wood Stove about breakfast. Sweet dreams, dear girl." She turned off the light and walked out of the room.

CHAPTER 9

The Golden Cord, Lullaby and Merlin

It was just before dawn when Aunt Edna came rushing back into Isobel's room crying, "Quick, dear, get up! We must go shopping for horses and we must do it now!" Isobel sat up as Aunt Edna began throwing clothes at her. "I think this and perhaps this and those shoes and..."

Aunt Edna stopped suddenly. "These won't do at all. You should have riding clothes. Yes, riding clothes. Now, where did I put those black riding trousers..." and she rushed out of the room.

Isobel turned on her bedside lamp, got out of bed and waited. She could hear Aunt Edna in the next room opening drawers and cupboards and throwing things around, all the time muttering, "Where are they? Everything's been moved around. Such a nuisance. Oh, where are..." There was a sudden whoop of joy and she rushed back into the bedroom holding up a handful of garments and a pair of boots. "I knew I had them somewhere! Look, my old riding habit! I've got trousers and a shirt and a jacket and hat and boots."

She was also holding something that Isobel didn't recognise. It looked like a row of ribs sown into some cloth with laces at either end. "What's that?"

"My old riding corset, of course." Aunt Edna held it out in front of her and frowned. "Hmm, perhaps not. Girls don't wear them anymore, do they? They were horribly hot, so probably not a good thing." She dropped the corset and thrust the other clothes at Isobel. "Quick now, we don't have a moment to spare. The Great Smoking Beastie is waiting for us," and she rushed out of the room again.

Isobel put the clothes on. They smelled of mothballs and looked rather odd. The black trousers were a bit stiff, the frilly white blouse had a high neck that came right up under her chin, and the black jacket with brass buttons down the front was very tight. The black boots came to her knees and had laces all the way up the front. The hat was a black top hat like the one Bert wore in the wedding picture. She looked at herself in the mirror. She looked very strange indeed, but everything fitted well enough.

Aunt Edna called her from the front veranda. She went outside with Diggidydog and Grumblebumkin at her heels.

The light was just beginning to change from grey to pink and Isobel could hear crows and magpies announcing the morning. The Great Smoking Beastie was idling in front of the house, a little stream of black smoke blowing out the back. Aunt Edna stood in the back of the ute with a long golden cord which she was tying to a hook on one side. The ghosts were sitting in their rocking chairs, watching Aunt Edna who looked up as Isobel came through the door. She suddenly clapped her hands and cried, "Well, look at you! I knew those clothes would come in handy again one day. Never pays to throw anything out."

Isobel went down the steps. "What are you doing, Aunt Edna?"

"Getting The Great Smoking Beastie ready for the family, of course." She ran the golden cord across to the other side of the ute, wrapped it around another hook, then did the same again with two more hooks so that there was a closed square of golden cord. "There's a breeze coming up, you see. Can you feel it?"

Isobel turned her face a little and felt a touch of breeze on her cheek. "Is that important?"

Aunt Edna shook her head. "My oh my, what do they teach children in school these days? Don't you know that ghosts don't like the wind? Even a little breeze will blow them all over the place. Goodness, I've seen them blown clear across the farm on a windy day. That's why ghosts like to live inside houses. No wind inside a house, is there? They could go out last night because it was perfectly still, but there is a breeze coming up this morning and the only way to stop them from blowing around is to keep them tied down with the golden cord."

Isobel touched the golden cord. It was heavy. "Is it real gold?"

"Of course. Won't work unless it's real gold. But not all of it, dear, otherwise I wouldn't be able to lift it, would I? It's rope with a lot of gold threads woven through it. You haven't seen one before?"

"No. Where did you get it?"

"From the Golden Cord Master. Where else does one buy golden cord? He's a funny little chap. Works out of an old tin shed behind a chocolate factory in Adelaide." Aunt Edna tied the last knot. "Now, get in. We don't have any time to waste." She jumped down from the back of the ute and got in behind the wheel. Isobel climbed in beside her.

The ghosts floated off their rocking chairs and sat themselves inside the square of golden cord. Diggidydog jumped up onto the back of the ute and sat with his head hanging over the side. Grumblebumkin leapt in through the window and wrapped himself around Aunt Edna's neck. She patted him fondly.

Isobel said. "Where are we going, Aunt Edna?"

"To the Chen's place first. Granny said there is a fine pony for you there, and Grandpa saw a perfect horse for me at Mr Mohamed's stud. Mr Mohamed is retiring and selling off his horses.

"Why are we in such a hurry?"

"Because there is a horse sale in Hopperfield today and the pony and the horse are both being sold off. We must buy them before the sale starts. Before they are even loaded up to be taken to the sale. Can't risk missing out. There's only one right horse for each person, you know. Another horse simply won't do." She took her knitting out of her handbag, banged on the dashboard of the ute and cried, "Go, Beastie!" The Great Smoking Beastie leapt forward and took off.

Isobel hung on to her seat as the The Great Smoking Beastie tore along the track to the front gate, then veered left and raced along the dirt road. She turned to look through the back window and saw Diggidydog with his face leaning into the wind, his toothless smile stretched into a big crazy grin with his lips flapping around his ears. Granny, Grandpa, Ma, Pa and Bert sat in the back of the ute, snugly contained within the square of golden cord. They looked quite comfortable. As she looked on, they hit a bump and Bert was flung out of the square, but he reached out and grabbed the cord just in time. They hit another bump and the other four ghosts grabbed onto the rope as they were sucked out of the square, their ghostly bodies flying out behind the ute like streamers. Isobel cried, "They're out!"

Aunt Edna looked up from her knitting. "Are they hanging on?"

"Yes, but…"

"Don't worry, they'll be alright. Can't hurt a ghost, can you?" She went back to her knitting.

"What happens if they let go?"

"Oh they'll blow around the paddocks for awhile, but they always make their way home in the end."

Isobel watched Aunt Edna knit for a moment. "Shouldn't you be steering, Aunt Edna?"

"Oh no, The Great Smoking Beastie knows where to go. Besides, I don't know how to drive. Never learned, you see."

"Oh."

"You should learn, though. I could ride a horse before I could walk and I was driving a horse and cart at your age. You should know how to drive a car, being a modern girl and all that. The Great Smoking Beastie will show you how."

"Really?"

"Really."

Isobel thought about that as they bounced and bumped along. Staying with Aunt Edna was a lot of fun. "How come you own a car that doesn't need you to steer it?"

"I don't own the Great Smoking Beastie, dear, it owns me. It found me and decided I was the right person to live with and now I belong to it."

"How did it find you?"

Aunt Edna looked up from her knitting and smiled wistfully as she remembered. "It was the day Sir Galahad died. He was my horse for thirty years and I did love him so. Great big old grey, he was, with hairy feet and a tangled mane. He loved to gallop and so did I. We rode into town one day to get some groceries and were walking up the main street when he stopped dead. Just like that." Aunt Edna sighed.

"Why did he stop?"

"Like I said. Dead. Right there in the middle of the street, standing up with me on his back and a basket of apples and bananas on my lap."

"Oh. That's sad."

"He'd had a good life. It was his time."

"Did he go transparent?"

"No, only humans go transparent when it's their time."

"What happened then?"

"Well, I got off and people started gathering around. Someone said we should get him off the street, but we couldn't move him. He just stood there like a statue with his eyes closed, dead as a doornail and going nowhere. Next thing I know, someone drove up in a crane and Sir Galahad was lifted up and carried away. And there I was, standing in the street with my shopping basket and a saddle and no way to get home. Then I heard a car horn and looked around to see The Great Smoking Beastie parked down a side street next to the butcher shop. I walked over to see who was honking the horn, but there wasn't anyone there. Mr Fraser, the butcher, came out and asked me why I'd honked the horn. I said I hadn't, it had honked by itself. He didn't believe me, but then it honked again and made us both jump. Must be a loose wire, Mr Fraser said and he lifted the bonnet. Funny, he said, there's no battery, so the horn shouldn't be working. It honked again and he banged his head on the bonnet. Then the motor started up and Mr Fraser nearly jumped out of his skin. He said that old car hadn't worked for twenty years and he was quite befuddled by it. Said he couldn't fix it, nobody wanted to buy it, he couldn't even sell it to the junk yard. No one wanted an old 1934 Ford Utility with more rust than paint on it. So it just sat in that little side street going rustier with each year and making the place look untidy. I said I'd buy it if someone could teach me to drive. He said I could have it for nothing if I'd just take it away. Of course

I said 'yes please' and he went to fetch the keys. I sat inside it to see what it felt like and it suddenly took off, turned up the main street and didn't stop until I got home. Knew where I lived, clever little Beastie. Mr Fraser came the next day with the keys, but I've never needed them. Dear little Beastie starts up whenever it feels like it and whenever I need to use it and all it ever wants is a feed of petrol and water and a bit of oil from time to time."

"How do you know it will show me how to drive?"

"Oh it likes you, dear. It wouldn't let you in if it didn't." Aunt Edna patted the dashboard fondly. "Isn't that right, Beastie?" A sweet purring sound came from under the bonnet for a brief moment before the engine resumed its usual roar. Isobel thought it was a very nice ute indeed.

They drove on for half an hour as the sun broke over the horizon and the landscape was cast into long morning shadows. It was very bumpy and noisy inside the ute, with the wind whistling past them, the roar of the engine and an occasional explosion of black smoke out the back. Aunt Edna had her head down and seemed happy with her knitting, so Isobel just looked around and wondered what would happen next.

The Great Smoking Beastie suddenly veered sharply to the right and passed through a gate with the name 'Wei and Xui Ying Chen' on it. Another ten minutes of rattling along and they came to a big modern farmhouse surrounded by sheds and stables. A dozen ponies grazed in a nearby paddock and two big dogs stood near the house, their ears forward as they watched The Great Smoking Beastie come to a sudden halt by the house. The dogs didn't bark, they just stared, mainly at the ghosts. The ghosts settled back into their golden square and stared back at the dogs.

A man came onto the front veranda with a steaming cup of tea in his hand. He was tall and slender and wore jeans and a red t-shirt. "Aunt Edna?" he said with surprise. "What are you doing here?"

Aunt Edna unwrapped Grumblebumkin from her neck, put him on the dashboard and got out of the car. "I'm here to buy a pony for my niece, Mr Chen."

"Oh. Well, I've got quite a good selection…"

"It has to be Lullaby."

"Lullaby? She's going to the sale today. I've already got a possible buyer lined up for her…"

"I know all that. I know she's won prizes in jumping and dressage and cross-country. She's a fine pony. I'll give you double what that buyer has offered. I'll give you $24,800."

Mr Chen's eyes opened wide. "How do you know how much I've been offered? I only spoke to him last night."

"Someone told me, it doesn't matter who. Will you accept my offer?"

"That's a lot of money, even for a champion jumper like Lullaby."

"She's worth it. We'll take her now, if you don't mind, as we have another horse to buy before the sale and we must get on."

"You mean...right now?"

"Yes, right now."

Mr Chen looked into the car and said to Isobel sitting there in her top hat, "Don't you want to meet Lullaby first? See if you get on alright with her?"

Before Isobel could respond, Aunt Edna said, "Oh, she'll get on just fine with her. I've had it on good authority that Lullaby is the right pony for Isobel." She reached into her handbag and pulled out some money. A lot of money. "Here you are. $25,000 and you can keep the change."

Mr Chen nearly dropped his cup of tea. "You don't waste any time, do you? There's some paperwork to do..."

"Drop it into Hopperfield Station when you get time. You know where it is."

Mr Chen took the pile of cash and stared at it. "Don't you at least want a receipt?"

"Bring it with you when you come. For now, just get Lullaby and tie her to the back of the ute, will you? She can follow us home." Aunt Edna started to get back in the car, then stopped. "Oh, I need some hay. Do you have any?"

"Of course. I'll throw a few bales in the back of the ute. And some oats. Have you got a saddle for your niece?"

"A saddle? I've got several, but they're a bit old and need a good oiling. Haven't been into my stables for many, many years. Everything is there, it just needs a clean up."

"I've got a saddle for sale, should be about right for your niece. I'll throw that in with the hay and oats. I've got some other riding tack for Lullaby that you can have as well. And…" Mr Chen looked in at Isobel again. "…and I've got some of my daughter's riding clothes that she grew out of last year. They should fit Isobel nicely."

"She has my old riding clothes. She's wearing them."

Mr Chen smiled. "I can see that. They're a little old fashioned, Aunt Edna, and that hat is no longer appropriate. She needs an approved hard riding hat. I'll get my daughter's things for her."

"Well, if you must. But we're in a terrible hurry. Need to drop in on Mr Mohamed on the way home."

"I'll be quick."

It only took a few minutes to get the clothes from the house, the saddle and horse tack from the stables, and the hay from the hay shed which he tied down with the golden cord in the back of the ute. The ghosts ducked as the hay bales were thrown in, but the bales passed straight through them, leaving their heads sticking out of the top. He dropped the oats and some other feed into the remaining space and Diggidydog was forced to jump into the front seat next to Isobel. Finally he fetched Lullaby from the paddock. She came as soon as Mr Chen whistled. He tethered her to the back of the ute and waved Aunt Edna off. Aunt Edna kept her hands on the steering wheel, pretending to drive, until they passed through the gate and then she took her knitting out again. Grumblebumkin lay stretched out on the dashboard, his blazing green eyes watching the road ahead while Diggidydog hung his head out the window to catch the breeze in the way that dogs do.

Isobel could not take her eyes off Lullaby. The pony was brown with a white star on her forehead. Her coat was shiny and her eyes bright. Isobel couldn't wait to meet her properly. For now, Lullaby followed The Great Smoking Beastie along the road, although they travelled at a slower pace than before. A pony can only trot so fast.

The ghosts were sitting inside the hay bales with only their bobbing heads visible, and they were all grinning at Lullaby.

As they drove on, Aunt Edna put her hand on the dashboard and said softly, "Now, you know I'm getting a horse for myself today, little Beastie. I'm only getting it because it can gallop and you can't. You can go fast, but you can't gallop or jump over fences. I don't want you getting jealous and giving me a hard time about it. Are you going to be alright with that?"

The Great Smoking Beastie purred again and Aunt Edna smiled.

Soon, they turned into another gate and came to a large old stone house set in a garden of big trees and sweeping lawns. Behind it was a long stable and a racing track surrounded by a white fence. There were training yards and pens, but Isobel could not see any horses. Three dogs came out of the stable as they pulled up in front of the house. A man followed them. He was short with dark grey hair, a big moustache and skinny legs.

Aunt Edna got out of the car. The man said, "Hello, Aunt Edna. I wasn't expecting you this morning."

"Hello, Mr Mohamed. Thought I'd just pop in unannounced, as I always do. Goodness, your place looks almost deserted since I was last here."

"Yes, I've sold most of the stock and the new owners will be here in a month with their own. I'm retiring to the coast. Looking forward to it." Mr Mohamed looked at Lullaby. "Nice little pony you've got there."

"Indeed. We've just bought her from Mr Chen. And I'm here to buy Merlin."

Mr Mohamed looked even more surprised than Mr Chen had.

"You want Merlin? You can look him over at the sales later today. I'm taking the last five horses into town and expecting buyers for all of them. I'll be there by lunch time…"

"Oh no, I must have him now. He's a racer, isn't he? Won the Melbourne Cup a few years back?"

"Quite a few years back. But he was injured shortly afterwards and hasn't raced since. There is a buyer in Adelaide interested in him."

"What sort of buyer?"

"It's a riding school."

"A riding school? You mean where they put children on horses and go round and round in circles all day?"

"Yes. Not a bad retirement for an old racer."

"Oh dear, that won't do at all. I have it on good authority that Merlin likes to run."

"He does indeed, but there's no money in it any more. His racing days are over."

"I'm not interested in racing or money, Mr Mohamed. I want him for myself. I want a good runner."

Mr Mohamed looked doubtful. "He's a big horse, Aunt Edna, and quite a handful."

"I like big horses. Sir Galahad was 18 hands. Merlin is only 17 hands. He'll suit me very nicely. I'll give you $10,000 for him."

Mr Mohamed's eyes nearly popped. "Whaaaat? That much? Why that's more than twice what I was expecting. Well, it's hardly worth taking him to the sale if you're offering that much for him. You've got a deal. When do you want him?"

Aunt Edna reached into her handbag once more and took out another pile of money. "Right now. Here's your money. You can drop by Hopperfield Station with the paperwork and the receipt when you're ready. Just get him and tie him to the back of the ute, will you?"

Mr Mohamed was speechless. He took the money and walked into the stable shaking his head. When he came back, he was leading a big black horse with four white feet and a long silky black mane. He tethered Merlin behind the ute next to Lullaby. "Are you sure about this, Aunt Edna?"

"Absolutely."

"You don't want to try him out…"

"I can see just by looking at him that we are made for each other. Now I must away as I've things to do. Nice doing business with you."

"And with you."

Aunt Edna put her hands on the steering wheel and they drove away. Isobel looked behind her and saw Mr Mohamed still shaking his head as he counted the money in his hands. He looked up as they went through the gate and waved.

Aunt Edna drove along the road for about a mile, then suddenly cried, "Stop!" The Great Smoking Beastie stopped in the middle of the road.

Isobel said, "Why have we stopped? Is something wrong?"

"No, dear. The horses are nicely warmed up and I can't wait any longer. We are both going to ride back home. Hop out."

They got out of the car. The ghosts watched from the safety of their golden cord, for it was quite windy now. Aunt Edna quickly saddled Lullaby, pulled the reins over the pony's head and said, "Time to meet your Lullaby. On you get."

Isobel took the top hat off, put Mr Chen's daughter's hard hat on and mounted the pony. "She's perfect, Aunt Edna. Just perfect."

"Of course she is, dear. Never question a ghost's judgement. And you look quite marvellous up there in my old riding things. Pity about the silly hat, though. Oh well."

"What are you going to do? You don't have a saddle."

"I don't need a saddle. I prefer riding bareback. I can feel the horse better that way."

"What about driving back? Do we leave the ute here?"

"Oh goodness no. The Great Smoking Beastie knows its way back home. It can follow us."

Aunt Edna walked to the fence by the side of the road and opened a gate. "We'll go across the paddocks. If you can't keep up, just follow Beastie home. Alright?"

"Sure. But won't the farmer mind us going through his paddocks?"

"I'm the farmer. It's all my land this side of the road." She went to Merlin and put her face against his. "You're a lovely old thing, aren't you? When was the last time you had a really good gallop, hey? Fancy one now?" Merlin neighed and his top lip curled back. Isobel thought it looked just like a smile. He stamped his foot on the ground and rested his big head on Aunt Edna's shoulder. "Thought so. It's been a while for me too."

Aunt Edna led Merlin through the gate and waited while Isobel and The Great Smoking Beastie followed. Grumblebumkin slid onto the driver's seat and put his paws on the steering wheel, looking for all the world like he was driving. Diggidydog slumped against the car door with his face hanging out.

Aunt Edna shut the gate and leapt up onto Merlin's back. She was old and short and Merlin was big and strong, but when she leapt up it was like she had springs in her legs. She settled herself on his back, took her teeth out and popped them into her pocket, jammed her hat down on her head, leaned forward with her fingers entwined in the black mane and cried, "Come on, old fellow, let's run!"

Merlin leapt forward as if he was in the starting gate at the Melbourne Cup Races. Isobel and Lullaby galloped after him for a little while, but it was clear very quickly that they had no hope of keeping up. Merlin was galloping at full speed with Aunt Edna sitting low behind his head like a jockey. Isobel could not believe how fast they were. She slowed Lullaby to a comfortable trot behind The Great Smoking Beastie and watched as Aunt Edna and Merlin approached the paddock fence in the distance. She thought they might stop and open a gate, but instead Merlin and Aunt Edna rose into the air, flew over the fence with a cry of "Yeehaa!" and disappeared over the crest of a hill.

The ghosts' heads were bobbing along in the back of the ute, watching Isobel and Lullaby with approving faces. Grumblebumkin kept his paws on the steering wheel and Diggidydog stared ahead with his flapping toothless grin. The Great Smoking Beastie idled along happily, taking care not to backfire and frighten Lullaby.

Isobel looked around her at the wide brown paddocks and big blue sky and thought it might just be the best place in the world.

CHAPTER 10

Tiaras for Breakfast and Being a Ghost

When they got back, The Great Smoking Beastie parked close to the front veranda. The ghosts rose out of the hay bales and shot into the house before the wind could get hold of them. Aunt Edna was around the shady side of the house with Merlin. He was drinking from a horse trough while she cooled him down with a wet sponge. As Isobel and Lullaby arrived, she said, "Tether Lullaby here, dear. She'll need a drink and a sponge, too." When they were done, Aunt Edna filled two buckets with feed and put them in front of the horses.

"Time for our feedbags now." She hung her hat on the hook by the door, slipped her boots off and went inside.

Isobel left her boots next to Aunt Edna's and went into the passage. She could hear Aunt Edna tossing things around inside her bedroom again and wondered what she was looking for this time. Aunt Edna came out wearing a diamond tiara on her head and a long diamond and sapphire necklace around her neck. "It's time for a celebration and we always dress for dinner with the family," she said, "even when it's breakfast." She held another tiara and necklace in her hand. She took Isobel's hat off and said, "Hats for outdoors, tiaras for indoors, dear." Isobel put the tiara and necklace on and looked at herself in the passage mirror. She thought she looked very sparkly indeed.

Isobel was expecting to go out onto the back veranda, but instead Aunt Edna led her into the kitchen. It wasn't too hot in there yet, despite Barking Wood Stove sizzling away. In fact, it was cosy and bright and smelled delicious. The kitchen table was set for seven with a linen tablecloth, fine china plates, polished silver cutlery and crystal glasses full of orange juice. The ghosts were sitting around the table, their knives and forks floating above their plates, even though their hands were folded neatly in their laps. Isobel sat down.

Barking Wood Stove woofed and Aunt Edna took a big casserole dish out of the oven. She spooned cheesy tuna, cherry and broccoli casserole onto each plate, poured herself a cup of tea and sat down. She said, "Two four six eight, bog in, don't wait," and everyone started to eat.

Isobel tasted her green and red and brown casserole. It looked ghastly, but was delicious. The ghosts' knives and forks picked up the food and put it in the their mouths. Up and down those knives and forks went, but sometimes they missed the mouths and the food went where the eyes were or the chins. When Grandpa turned his head to look at Isobel, the food went in through his ear. It didn't seem to matter, for the food just dropped straight through them. They kept eating and the food piled up on the chairs. Isobel was staring at them when Grandpa said, "What are you looking at, child?"

"Can you taste it? The food?"

"Of course we can. Ghosts can taste. Didn't you know that?"

"No."

Aunt Edna said, "I don't think her school teaches anything about ghosts. She didn't know about the golden cord."

Granny said, "Well, neither did I when I was her age. Didn't really learn about it until we were on the Other Side. Perhaps this is a good time for a lesson about ghosts. What would you like to know about ghosts, Isobel?"

"Everything, please."

All the ghosts started talking at the same time.

"We can taste and smell and hear and see. We just can't touch anything. Quite a nuisance, actually."

"But we can move things. Small things.

"We can't move big things. That takes a special sort of ghost. That takes a poltergeist, but they can be quite naughty at times, tripping people up and throwing things around a room to get attention. You would never invite a poltergeist to a party."

"We don't feel the heat or the cold. That can be quite nice, especially when there is a frost outside."

"Or a heat wave."

"But we don't like the wind."

"We can go wherever we want, as long as there is no wind."

"The wind is our enemy."

"When it's not windy, we can travel long distances in the blink of an eye. Whoosh and we're all over the place. That can be fun."

"We can visit people, see who is new in the district and how they're getting on."

"We can see if someone is happy or sad or in love or worried or having money problems."

"Edna sends us on missions. We find out what is going on and report back to her. Then she can do something to help."

"But we can't read minds. No, that would be rude."

"We can go through walls..."

"...but it makes us dizzy. Well, it would, wouldn't it? All that stone and brick and timber rattling around inside your head."

"No, best to go through a door if there is one. We can open doors..."

"...as long as the door isn't too big. And we only need to open it a crack to slip through."

"We don't feel pain..."

"... get tired..."

"...or feel angry."

"But we do like a good laugh..."

"...and we do get annoyed."

They stopped suddenly and looked at Isobel whose head had been turning from side to side as she tried to keep up. It was a lot to take in. She thought a moment, then said, "What annoys you?"

Ma said, "Only the usual sorts of things. Fat vampires. Werewolves with fleas. Whispering banshees. Zombies who forget where they are buried. You know. The usual stuff."

Isobel shook her head. "I don't know about any of that."

Aunt Edna put her knife and fork on her empty plate and said, "You soon will, dear. Have you finished your casserole?"

"Yes."

"Wonderful!" Aunt Edna leapt up and took a big chocolate cake from the sideboard. It had green icing and sticks of celery poking out of it. "Time for dessert." She cut slices for everyone and poured herself another cup of tea.

Isobel had never seen celery sticks in chocolate cake or green broccoli icing before, but it all tasted perfect. She watched as the piles of food on the ghost's chairs got bigger and wetter and sloppier with each mouthful of food and orange juice, and then breakfast was over and Aunt Edna slapped her knee and said, "Right! Time to get those little trees into the ground before it gets too hot." She rushed out of the kitchen, calling over her shoulder, "Leave the plates, Isobel. Grumbly will clean them and the family will tidy up. Put some shorts on and come outside. We have work to do!"

Isobel wondered if Aunt Edna ever slowed down. It was hard keeping up.

CHAPTER 11

Little Trees, Timid Snakes and Grateful spiders

Isobel changed into shorts and t-shirt and went outside, but she couldn't see Aunt Edna. Then she heard The Great Smoking Beastie start up behind the house and followed the noise. Aunt Edna was loading trays of plants into the back of the ute next to one of the big sheds. The plants were little trees, each one in its own small black pot. Diggidydog and Grumblebumkin were watching her from the shade of the pepper tree. Aunt Edna got in the ute and called out, "Get in, dear! Much to do! Diggidy, guard the house! Grumbly, clean the plates!" Diggidydog flopped on the veranda and Grumblebumpkin went inside.

Isobel got into the car. Aunt Edna handed her a small spade. "This should do you."

"What's this for?"

"Digging holes, of course."

Aunt Edna slapped the dashboard, The Great Smoking Beastie belched black smoke and took off.

"Where are we going, Aunt Edna?"

"To the back paddock today."

"Why? What's there?"

"Nothing. That's why we're going there."

"Are we going to plant the little trees?"

"Of course. What else would you do with little trees?" Aunt Edna grinned.

"OK." Isobel grinned back.

The Great Smoking Beastie roared across the empty paddocks until they came to a paddock full of tall trees with different coloured barks and arching branches. It was shady and cool as they drove between the trees. The first trees were very big, but as they drove along the trees got smaller and smaller until they came to a gate. On the other side of the gate was a big empty paddock. Aunt Edna said, "See? Nothing here. A nice fresh paddock to start planting up. We can call this one Isobel's Back Paddock. Would you like that?"

Isobel nodded happily. She'd never had a paddock named after her before. She got out of the ute and looked back. The trees behind them looked like a great green wave that peaked in the distance. They smelled of eucalyptus and she could hear parrots, cockatoos and magpies. It had been lovely in there, but here in the empty paddock, it was already hot and dusty.

Aunt Edna was unloading the ute. "Give us a hand, dear."

Isobel threw herself into the work. They dug holes and planted the little trees, stepping out the distance between each. "Five big strides for me, ten strides for your short little legs, Isobel." When they were all in the ground, Aunt Edna filled two watering cans from a big container and they watered each of the trees. Isobel thought they looked very neat in their orderly rows. She counted them. They had planted a hundred trees.

Then Aunt Edna said, "Time to get back. It's still early and we need to clean out a couple of stalls for Merlin and Lullaby. Been such a long time since I was in the stables. Who knows what we'll find in there."

They roared and bounced back to the house where the ghosts were peering through the kitchen window. It was too windy to leave the house.

Aunt Edna unloaded the empty pot trays and they went to the stables.

Isobel was used to the stables at school. They were hot in the summer and cold in the winter, with low roofs and small stalls. She gasped when she saw Aunt Edna's stables. The walls were thick stone and the roof soared high above them. There were two rows of stalls either side of a long corridor. A ladder led up to a hay loft at one end and old saddles and riding tack hung from the walls. It smelled of musty hay and dried manure and was cool, despite the heat building up outside.

Aunt Edna stood in the middle of the stables with her hands on her hips and looked around. "Now, which stalls will they like, hey? Perhaps we should let them choose."

"I'll get them, Aunt Edna."

Isobel ran to the house, untethered Merlin and Lullaby and led them to the stables. Aunt Edna stroked the horses and said, "Pick your new home, dearies."

Merlin looked around, then walked over to a stall halfway along. He rested his head on the gate and neighed.

Aunt Edna said, "That one for you, then. Now it's Lullaby's turn."

Lullaby walked straight to the stall directly opposite Merlin and whinnied.

Aunt Edna said, "Good choice. The two of you can chat while you're in here." She picked up a rake. "Take Merlin and Lullaby outside while we muck out the stalls, Isobel. There's an exercise yard behind the stables. Don't forget to shut the gate."

Isobel took the two horses outside and remembered to shut the gate. She found another rake by the stable door and went into Lullaby's stall. She started to drag a pile of rotting hay towards her when a snake suddenly raised its head just a few feet away and looked right at her. She screamed and jumped back. The snake also jumped back.

Aunt Edna rushed to her side. "What is it? What's wrong?"

"Snake!"

Aunt Edna looked over the stall gate and calmly said, "Oh, it's just a black snake. He won't harm you. You probably gave him a fright."

"But it's a snake!"

"And a fine big chap he is too. A good six feet I would say." Aunt Edna turned towards the snake and said sweetly, "I'm sorry we disturbed you, little snakey. If we'd known you were there, we would have asked you to leave first."

The snake moved his head up and down as if he understood every word Aunt Edna was saying.

Isobel cried, "But it's a snake and I hate snakes! I'm scared of snakes!"

Aunt Edna patted her on the arm. "I know, dear, so many people are. But they are more frightened of you than you are of them. Snakes are really rather helpless. They're so little and they don't have any arms or legs. Can you imagine how hard that is, trying to catch your dinner and eat it without arms or legs? And they are so low to the ground, people don't see them. They keep running over the poor dears and squashing them. No, it's a hard life being a snake." She turned back to the snake. "But you can't stay here, little snakey, not now that we are moving horses back in. You know that, so off you go. You've got 50,000 acres to play in, so go play."

The snake slithered out of the stall. Aunt Edna looked around her and said, very loudly, "And that goes for any other snakes in here! Time for you to move on!"

Isobel watched with wide, frightened eyes as a dozen snakes came from every direction and slithered down the corridor and out of the stables. Brown snakes, black snakes, tiger snakes, copperheads and pythons.

Aunt Edna looked around her again. "Lets see what else is in here, shall we?" She put her hands on her hips again and cried, "Right! I want spiders in the Spider House! Possums outside up trees! Mice and rats in the empty sheds! Wombats and kangaroos in the paddocks! Birds back in the trees where you belong! Have you all got that? Move!"

There was rustling and rattling, a flapping of wings and scuttling of feet as creatures great and small moved out of their webs and nests and holes towards the stable doors. Isobel stood on the stall gate and watched them go past. When she saw the spiders, she stepped higher onto the gate. She hated spiders almost as much as she hated snakes. There were so many! Redbacks, huntsmen, trapdoors, white-tails, black house spiders, fat brown spiders, daddy-long-legs, golden orb spiders and wolf spiders. And they were all in a hurry. They moved around Aunt Edna as she waved them this way and that like a policeman directing traffic.

A big hairy spider dropped from the roof and landed on Aunt Edna's shoulder. Isobel gasped and said, "Look out, Aunt Edna, there's one on you!"

Aunt Edna glanced down at the fat huntsman and said gently, "No, little one, you can't stay in here. You'll be very lonely if you do. You go to the Spider House with your friends and have some fun. I always leave the windows open and there are plenty of flies in there for you to eat." The spider raised one of its hairy legs and stroked Aunt Edna's cheek, then jumped onto the floor and scuttled out of the stable.

A loud hoot above them made Isobel jump. She looked up and saw two big barn owls roosting on the roof beam above her head. Three little baby owls sat next to them. Aunt Edna looked up. "Oh alright, Mr and Mrs Owl, you can stay. Don't want to upset little Hoot, Howl and Holler, do we? But you will hunt in the other sheds, not in here. Understood?" The owls nodded and hooted their appreciation.

Isobel said, "They can understand you? The snakes and the owls and the spiders?"

"Of course, dear. They know who is boss."

Isobel shuddered. "Spiders creep me out, Aunt Edna."

"Oh no, dear, they're lovely little things. So clever and artistic. They make the most beautiful webs and no one teaches them how to spin them. They just do it. Marvellous little critters." Aunt Edna frowned. "But I don't like them in the house. I don't want to accidentally step on them or find them spinning their lovely webs behind the furniture. They have their very own house to live in these days. It used to be the old washhouse, but now that I have an inside laundry, the dear little creatures use it exclusively as a Spider House."

"Wow. That is so cool."

"Cool? Are you cold, dear?"

"No, cool. Like...wow, it's really good."

"Oh. Very well."

They watched the last of the critters leave the stable and Aunt Edna said, "Good. Now we can get to work."

They cleaned out the two stalls and spread fresh hay. Aunt Edna took all the old hay and manure around to the vegetable garden in a wheelbarrow. "The broccoli will love this," she said as she spread it on the ground. Then she filled the water troughs and Isobel brought the feedbags into the stalls. Aunt Edna looked around her and said with satisfaction, "That's a good start. We'll do some more this afternoon. It's time for morning tea. Bert likes his morning tea and it's cool in the freezer. Proper cool. Like...cold."

"The freezer?"

"Yes, dear. Would you like to join us?"

"With Frozen Bert?"

"Yes. I was thinking some broccoli and salmon custard tarts and cold lemonade."

"Alright."

They went back to the house. As they passed the old washhouse that was now the Spider House, Isobel looked in through one of the open windows. There were hundreds of spider webs criss-crossing the Spider House and too many spiders to count. As she peered in, she was sure every one of those spiders turned and looked at her with bright little eyes. She jumped back. Aunt Edna might think spiders were nice little critters, but she was not so sure.

CHAPTER 12

Morning Tea with Frozen Bert and a Call to Mr Hamble

Aunt Edna took green custard tarts and lemonade out of the fridge, put them on a tray with three glasses and led Isobel out to the freezer. She kicked the freezer door and it creaked open. They stepped inside.

Isobel wasn't sure what she was going to find, but it just looked like an ordinary freezer with shelves on either side. There were frozen peas and beans and blueberries and icecream and fish fingers and lamb chops and bacon and sausages and oven fries and bread and broccoli. Lots of broccoli. Bags and bags of frozen broccoli.

At the end of the freezer was a plain looking wall, but when Aunt Edna gave it a nudge, it swung open.

Frozen Bert sat strapped into his wheelchair looking straight ahead, very upright, very respectable in his blue striped pyjamas and slippers. His sunglasses sat perched on his nose and Isobel could see a little of his black eyes behind them. They looked spooky. There was a small table and chair in front of him. Aunt Edna put the tray on the table, lay a tea towel on the frozen chair and sat down. She looked around her. "There's a stool under the frozen peas, dear. You can sit on that."

Isobel got the stool and sat next to Aunt Edna. It was very cold.

Aunt Edna poured lemonade into the glasses, put one in front of Bert and gave the other to Isobel. She said, "Bert, dear, this is Isobel, Thomas's great granddaughter."

Isobel almost expected Frozen Bert to open his mouth and say something, but of course he didn't. He was dead. She said, "Does Ghost Bert come in here, too?"

"Goodness, no. He's quite cross about me keeping Bert here. Wants me to bury him. Says Frozen Bert should be in the graveyard with Ma and Pa and Granny and Grandpa, under his own headstone with flowers on his grave. Ghosts are like that. They like to be neat about things, you see. Bodies in the graveyard. Ghosts on the Other Side. All very proper."

"Why do you keep him if you've got Ghost Bert to talk to?"

Aunt Edna sighed a big sigh as she pushed a green tart towards Frozen Bert. "Well, dear, sometimes I like to talk to a person I can't see through. Someone solid, like me. It's company. It stops me from feeling alone. And it's nice to have morning tea with him. We used to do that on the back veranda a lot. It was our favourite thing and here we are still doing it a hundred years later."

"But he can't talk back like Ghost Bert, can he?"

"I know, but you can't have everything, can you?"

Isobel slipped her hand into Aunt Edna's. "And you're not alone any more. You have me now, Aunt Edna."

"Goodness, I do, don't I?" Aunt Edna squeezed Isobel's hand and took a big bite of her green custard tart. "But you're going back to school in Sydney. What will I do then?"

Isobel thought about that for a moment. "I don't like that school. I like it here."

"You don't like school? Why not?"

"They're not very friendly. Or interesting. Not like here where everything is interesting. And they all have Mums and Dads and go home in the holidays. I feel sad there all the time. Do I have to go back, Aunt Edna?"

"Why, my dear, of course not. I can't have you feeling sad. And I would be sad if you went back. We have a perfectly good school in Hopperfield and the school bus goes right past our gate. I would be delighted if you stayed here. What do you think about that, Bert?"

Frozen Bert stared back behind his sunglasses.

"He likes that, Isobel."

"How can you tell?"

"His sunglasses fall off when he doesn't like something."

"Then I don't have to go back?"

"No, you don't. I shall arrange it with Mr Hamble."

"So I really can stay?"

"Of course."

Isobel felt a huge sadness leave her and smiled. "This is so cool."

"So it is, so it is. Well, lets have some lemonade to celebrate before our noses freeze and fall off, then I'll go make a phone call to Mr Hamble."

"And you can bury Frozen Bert, now that I'm here and you've got someone solid to talk to."

Aunt Edna paused thoughtfully, then sipped her lemonade and said, "I can indeed. Would you like to be buried, Bert?"

Bert's sunglasses did not move.

"Very well, burying it is. But we'll have to do it quietly. Everyone else thinks he is already in the graveyard. Perhaps tonight, when the rest of Hopperfield is asleep."

"I can help."

"Why, thank you, dear. You're a good girl. Now, let's go. I can't feel my feet any more."

They went inside and Aunt Edna made her phone call with the ghosts gathered around her. She spoke for a few minutes, then turned to Isobel and said, "Well, that's all decided. Just one more piece of paper to sign and you're all mine. Now, go wash up and we'll make lunch."

Aunt Edna made sardine and apple sandwiches and iced broccoli tea for lunch and they sat on the back veranda, grinning at each other. It was very windy outside, so the ghosts stayed inside, but Isobel could see them peering through the window. They were grinning, too. It seemed everyone was happy about her staying.

As they finished lunch they heard Diggidydog's visitor bark. Aunt Edna said, "Who can that be?" They went onto the front veranda and waited. After a while, they saw two trucks coming up the track. When they stopped in front of the house, Mr Mohamed got out of one and Mr Chen got out of the other. There were two other men and three women with them.

Mr Mohamed came up the steps and said, "I saw Mr Chen at the horse sale, Aunt Edna. We decided to help you get your stables ready. It's too much for you and your niece. We've brought our stable hands with us and everything we need, so just show us the way and we'll get on with it."

Aunt Edna clapped her hands together with delight and her teeth fell out. She popped them back in and said, "Oh, that is marvellous! A few helping hands will make short work of it. This way!" She showed them all to the stables and Isobel pitched in with the others. The stalls were mucked out, the feed bins and water troughs were filled and the saddles and riding tack cleaned, oiled and polished.

Aunt Edna jumped from job to job, pointing at what needed doing, giving her approval when it was done and grinning her big toothy grin all over the place. When they were finished inside the stables, they went outside and tidied up the exercise yards, fixed the fencing and made sure the gates closed properly. Merlin and Lullaby went into their new stalls and everyone stood around and admired their handiwork. It was nearly sunset when they left, with promises of more help and the use of their horse trucks if they were ever needed.

Isobel watched the two trucks disappear down the track, then went inside to help Aunt Edna with dinner. The ghosts were setting the big polished table in the dining room. Plates floated through the air, cutlery rose out of drawers, candles suddenly lit as ghostly hands were waved over them and flowers snapped off their stems in the garden and wafted through the window before falling into a vase.

Isobel thought the table looked very posh and it was all just for scrambled eggs on toast. But it was Aunt Edna's scrambled eggs on toast. Pieces of chocolate and garlic stuck up through the eggs and mashed broccoli was spread on the toast instead of butter. It tasted very grand and Isobel thought the broccoli and mustard milkshake afterward was just the thing to have in crystal glasses.

The sun went down, the moon rose and it was time to bury Frozen Bert.

CHAPTER 13

A Grave in a Grove by Moonlight

Getting Frozen Bert out of the freezer was the first problem. The wheelchair was frozen solid to the floor. Aunt Edna pushed and pulled, but to no avail. She got a bucket of hot water and threw it over the wheels, but the water froze instantly and made it worse. Isobel tried her hair dryer, but that didn't even make a dent in the ice under the wheels. Finally, Aunt Edna went to the shed and came back with a flame thrower. "I use this to back burn if there is a bushfire nearby," she said. "Stand back, Isobel."

Isobel stepped out of the freezer and watched as Aunt Edna lit up and directed the flame thrower at the wheels of the wheelchair. It sounded like a jet plane and the ghosts, who were looking through the kitchen window, put their fingers in their ears. It worked a treat and the ice around the wheels melted in an instant. Aunt Edna dropped the flame thrower before the wheels melted as well and quickly pushed the wheelchair out of the freezer. Bert's slippers and the bottom of his frozen pyjama pants were a little singed, but otherwise he was fine.

The second problem was getting Frozen Bert into The Great Smoking Beastie. Aunt Edna put a couple of planks of wood against the back of the ute and pushed the wheelchair up them, but they snapped under the weight and Frozen Bert crashed to the ground. She got two stronger planks and managed to push him up with lots of help from Isobel. She tied the wheelchair down with some ordinary rope, licked her finger and held it up. "Hmm, bit of a wind tonight." She picked up the golden cord and went inside with Isobel hot on her heels.

Back in the kitchen, Aunt Edna and Isobel tied Bert, Ma, Pa, Granny and Grandpa together with the golden cord and floated them outside to The Great Smoking Beastie. The golden cord was secured to the hooks in the back of the ute and the ghosts were ready to go to a funeral. But Aunt Edna was not. She said, "I must change into my funeral dress."

Isobel followed her into her bedroom and watched as Aunt Edna went through her wardrobes. "It's in here somewhere..." She found long red dresses and wide green dresses and lots of brown dresses that all looked the same, but they were not what she was looking for. Then she pulled out a black dress. It looked exactly like the brown dress she had on, only it was black. She smiled with satisfaction, then looked Isobel over. "Isobel, you should have a proper funeral dress, too. Look in that box over there, dear. You'll find a very nice black dress that should fit you."

Isobel went to the big box at the end of Aunt Edna's bed and lifted the lid. There were all sorts of fancy clothes in there. She looked through them until she found a black dress and pulled it out. It was long and lacy and had little diamond buttons down the front. Aunt Edna said, "I wore that when Granny died. I was just your age. There are some shoes in there, too." Isobel found them. They were elegant little ankle boots with black laces and pointy toes. Aunt Edna admired them, then said regretfully, "My fat feet won't fit into anything but my old boots these days. Oh well."

The two of them changed into their funeral dresses and Aunt Edna was heading out the door when she exclaimed, "Hats! We need funeral hats!" There were hat boxes on the tops of the wardrobes. She stood on a chair and looked in hat box after hat box. "Nope. Not that one. Wrong colour. This one has flowers on it. That one is too casual. Ahh, here they are!"

Aunt Edna put on a wide black hat with a heavy veil over the face and placed another smaller black hat with a sheer little face veil on Isobel. She stood back and looked at

Isobel. "Hmm, needs a little something extra, don't you think? A diamond or two or three, perhaps." She reached into her underwear draw and pulled out a few items. "No, bracelets won't do. They'll get in the way of our digging. Let me see...necklaces, tiaras? No, not today. Ahh, here we are. Brooches! The very thing." She pinned a fancy diamond brooch to Isobel's dress and another to her own dress. "Hmm, almost, but not quite. Fancy hats need fancy earrings," and two pairs of diamond earrings appeared from amongst the old grey underpants. She put small earrings on herself and a pair of long dangly earrings on Isobel. They were so long that they scratched Isobel's shoulders, but she thought they were very pretty and sparkly, so she didn't mind.

Aunt Edna checked their reflections in the mirror with satisfaction. "Now we are ready for a funeral." She clomped out of the house in her old brown boots and black funeral dress, calling out behind her, "Diggidydog! Grumblebumkin! Come on! Time to bury Bert!" Diggidydog jumped into the back of the ute and sat at Frozen Bert's feet. Grumblebumkin took up his place around Aunt Edna's neck. His orange and grey fur looked very smart against the black dress.

Aunt Edna threw a couple of shovels in the back and they were off.

The next problem was getting to the cemetery without being seen. The cemetery was on the other side of town. There was a full moon and

The Great Smoking Beastie was very noisy, but as they approached Hopperfield the motor changed to a purr and the ute cruised quietly along the main street. The Great Smoking Beastie didn't fire up again until they were well clear of any houses.

The cemetery wasn't fancy. It looked like a paddock with a lot of headstones scattered around. It was surrounded by a grove of big pine trees that swayed and danced in the wind. The moonlight cast silvery shadows across all the graves and Isobel thought it was magical. They drove through the cemetery and stopped at a fenced off section. There were three big headstones inside the fence. Aunt Edna took a torch and shone it on the headstones. One had Granny and Grandpa's names on it, one had Ma and Pa's names on it, and the other had Bert Toddleby's name on it, with an empty space below where Aunt Edna's name should have been. But of course, she was an Eternal and so her name was never going to be added. Isobel wondered why no one had ever noticed that.

Diggidydog jumped down from the ute and came to inspect the graves. Aunt Edna put Grumblebumkin on the ground and untied the golden cord from the ute. She floated the ghosts to the grave site where she tied them to the fence to stop them from blowing away. The ghosts shimmered and glowed in the moonlight as they looked on. There wasn't much they could do to help, but it seemed the right sort of place for a family of ghosts to spend some time.

Aunt Edna and Isobel started digging in front of Bert's headstone. The ground was soft and sandy and it didn't take too long to dig out all the top soil. The ghosts kept trying to give them instructions - "more to the left", "lean harder on the shovel", "throw the dirt further from the grave" - but the wind blew their whispery voices away and their words sounded like sighs.

Isobel was sweating when the shovel finally hit the coffin. She wanted to take her hat off, but Aunt Edna still had her hat on and Isobel thought it might not be proper to take it off. They were both covered in dirt and Isobel couldn't see Aunt Edna's face at all through the dusty veils. Aunt Edna, however, was undaunted and said, "Oh good. I was getting bored. Now we can get on with it." They cleared the last of the dirt away from the top of the coffin. Aunt Edna said, "Get me the rope and screwdriver from little Beastie, will you dear?"

Isobel climbed out of the grave and fetched the items. She watched as Aunt Edna removed the screws and loosened the lid of the coffin. Then they tied the rope around the lid and lifted it away. Six big rocks lay inside, just as Aunt Edna had placed them in 1910. She lifted them out one by one and passed them up to Isobel.

Aunt Edna pushed Frozen Bert down the planks and wheeled him to the side of the grave. They unbuckled the belt that held him in and lifted him out. Isobel's fingers turned blue with cold as she helped Aunt Edna lower the frozen body into the grave. They placed him carefully in the coffin. And there he stayed, sitting very upright with his hands in his lap and his sunglasses still perched on his nose.

Aunt Edna lifted her veil and frowned. "Bother." Frozen Bert was still frozen. His fingers and toes were thawing, but he was still as frozen as an ice cube everywhere else. He was not going to fit into the coffin like that.

Aunt Edna said, "You pull his legs, Isobel, and I'll try to flatten his head." They pushed and pulled and did their best to straighten him out, but as Aunt Edna had said on the Lightning Rock, frozen is frozen. Finally, they climbed out of the grave and sat down for a rest. "Nothing for it but to wait until he thaws out a bit."

Isobel said, "Should we sing a song or something? Isn't that what they do at funerals?"

"Have you been to a funeral before, dear?"

"No. Mum and Dad were cremated in England. All I got was their ashes in a funny looking vase. Mr Hamble put them in his safe."

Aunt Edna's eyes opened in surprise. "Oh no, that will not do at all. They are Hopperfields. They should be here." She thought for a moment. "Did your mother have a family?"

"No. Mum was an orphan. Like me."

Aunt Edna put her arm around Isobel and gave her a squeeze. "You aren't an orphan any more, are you? You've got me and Bert and Ma and Pa and Granny and Grandpa and Lullaby and Merlin and Diggidydog and Grumblebumkin. Hardly an orphan at all."

Isobel looked up at the ghosts who were all nodding and smiling. Their mouths were moving but she could not hear their words. It didn't matter because she knew they were kind words she wasn't hearing. No, she wasn't an orphan any more. She snuggled into Aunt Edna while they waited for Bert to thaw.

Aunt Edna said, "We should bring your Mum and Dad's ashes here and give them a proper farewell with a proper headstone."

"That would be so good, Aunt Edna."

"Now, let's sing a song, hey? Do you know a suitable funeral song to sing, dear?"

Isobel thought for a moment. She looked down at Frozen Bert in his thawing blue striped pyjamas, then said, "I know a song about jammies."

"Jammies? What is that? A song about jam?"

"No, not about jam. About jammies. You know. Pyjamas."

"Oooh. Jammies. I see. Well, that sounds like an interesting song. You'll have to teach me the words. Sing away."

Isobel lifted her veil and hummed a catchy tune, snapping her fingers and tapping her foot to the rhythm. She started to sing at the top of her squeaky little girl voice.

"His legs stick out of his jammies
Because he is so tall.
If he wiggles his bum too hard
Down to the ground they fall.

His slippers are gross and manky
Because of his big stinky feet.
It makes his Mum real cranky.
She wants his feet to smell sweet.

His Mum says his farts are rotten.
They smell like a long dead rat.
He says his Mum has forgotten
That her farts smell worse than that.

When he has a cold in the head
His nose is full of green snot.
If he blows his nose too hard
He covers the bed in grot.

Ooooooooohhhhhh!!!
Bums wriggle, feet stink,
Farts smell like a dead rat.
But green snot all over the bed,
There's nothing worse than that!"

Aunt Edna listened with wide, surprised eyes and open mouth. She looked at the equally surprised ghosts. They looked back at her. Then she burst into loud, cackley laughter. She laughed so hard, she cried. She said, "Sing it again!" So Isobel did.

Aunt Edna started to sing along with her at the top of her loud old lady voice. Soon, the paddocks rang with the words, "His nose was full of green snot" and Aunt Edna's hysterical cackling laughter. They sang it again and again as the moon crossed the sky and Bert started to sag in the coffin.

The ghosts joined in as Aunt Edna and Isobel danced around The Great Smoking Beastie singing, "His slippers are rotten and manky". The ute bounced up and down to the rhythm of the song as brown and black boots tapped out a beat on the dry ground.

They held their noses as they sang, "Mum says my farts are rotten." The ghosts bobbed up and down as Isobel's long earrings swayed and sparkled in the moonlight.

They wiggled their bums as they sang, "His legs stick out of his jammies." Diggidydog and Grumblebumkin wiggled their bums as well.

Suddenly, Isobel pointed into the grave and said, "Look!" While they had been singing, Frozen Bert had thawed. He was melting and lying flat in the coffin. He looked like ordinary dead Bert now.

Aunt Edna put her hands on her hips and looked down at him. "Well, it's about time."

Isobel said, "He looks kind of sad."

"Hmm. I wonder if he is. Shouldn't be. After all, he's been dead a long time, hasn't he? Shall we ask him?" Aunt Edna undid the golden rope from the fence and drew the ghosts towards the open grave. They looked down and a sigh rose up, but it wasn't a sad sigh. It was a satisfied sigh. Aunt Edna said, "Are you sad, Bert?"

Ghost Bert put his arm around Aunt Edna and said, "No, not at all. And I look very nice in my blue striped jammies. Thank you, Edna."

Aunt Edna rested her head on Bert's shoulder, although it went straight through so it looked like her head was in the middle of his chest. "You are very welcome, dearest."

Ma said, "Shouldn't we say a few words? If the Reverend was here, he'd say something."

Pa said, "Yes, say a few words, Edna."

"Very well. Mmm, let me think." Aunt Edna straightened up and put on a serious face. "I loved my Bert. He was a good husband, a good farmer, a good friend and he made me very happy. He still does, don't you, Bert?"

Ghost Bert nodded and grinned.

Then Aunt Edna shone the torch down on Thawed Bert and sang, "Bert's legs stick of his jammies." She started to giggle.

Ghost Bert giggled, too, and sang along. "Bert's slippers are rotten and manky..."

Ma, Pa, Granny and Grandpa sang, "... because of his big stinky feet."

Isobel joined in and they danced around the grave, singing at the top of their voices while Aunt Edna hung on to the golden cord. The ghosts flapped around in the wind behind her, waving their arms and legs as they danced their ghostly dance in the moonlight. Diggidydog and Grumblebumpkin jumped up and down, barking and meowing, and The Great Smoking Beastie rocked to the rhythm of the song

The light was beginning to change. Aunt Edna suddenly stopped singing and dancing and said, "It'll be sunrise soon. Come on, let's put the lid on and go home. Oh, this has been a fun funeral. Best funeral I've ever been to!"

It only took a minute to put the lid on the coffin and another half hour to fill in the grave and load the ghosts back onto The Great Smoking Beastie. Aunt Edna was in such a good mood that she sang all the way home. Well, almost all the way. She whispered, "Bert's legs stick out of his jammies" as they quietly passed through Hopperfield.

The sun was barely above the horizon when they got home. Isobel had a bath and Aunt Edna had a shower. Isobel changed into her pyjamas. She was very tired. Aunt Edna came out of her room in a clean brown dress and socks. She was carrying a tray of leftover cake and the teapot. "Come on, dear, we'll have a quick cuppa on the veranda before you go to bed, then you can sleep all day."

The ghosts were in their rocking chairs, the golden cord carefully tied to the backs of the chairs. Isobel yawned as she watched the sun rise higher in the sky and listened to the creak of the rocking chairs, the warbling of the magpies and the summer crow calls. Aunt Edna said, "We'll go into town tomorrow and buy you some new clothes, Isobel. And a proper hat, like mine. Can't have you running around in hand-me-downs all the time." But Isobel didn't hear her. She was already asleep in her chair. She didn't feel Aunt Edna lift her gently and carry her to the bedroom. She didn't see the ghosts hovering over her as they pulled the sheet up and plumped up her pillow. She just knew she was home.

CHAPTER 14

Mum and Dad in a Vase and Fat Baby Magpies

Isobel and Aunt Edna planted many trees in Isobel's Back Paddock over the next week. Isobel wore the new farm clothes and elastic-sided boots that Aunt Edna bought for her, which were all brown of course, and the new Akubra hat, which was exactly like Aunt Edna's and didn't blow off in the wind. They went out at sunrise when it was cool and came back to the house for morning tea. Then they went up to the waterhole for a swim.

After lunch, they worked in the stables and rode Merlin and Lullaby in the late afternoon when it was cooler. Aunt Edna showed Isobel around the farm and she learned to open and shut the paddock gates like a good country girl. But there was one paddock they didn't ride through. The gate was painted red with a big padlock hanging from it and the paddock was brown and flat. Aunt Edna said it was the Zombie Paddock and it wasn't polite to disturb sleeping zombies. Isobel was fine with that, for she wasn't too keen to meet any zombies anyway. They rode around the paddock instead.

She thought they must have covered the whole farm in that week, but of course 50,000 acres takes more than a week to ride around. Aunt Edna said she'd find the old tent she knew she had somewhere or other and they could go camping, as it would take a couple of days to reach the furthest paddocks.

Isobel liked it best when they rode through the forests that Aunt Edna had been planting for a hundred years. The horses walked through them slowly, making as little noise as possible. There were birds and animals and sweet smelling leaves and a special sort of muffled silence that made the birdcalls sound like bells. There were creeks and little waterfalls that Aunt Edna said had not been there before the trees were planted. Isobel thought they were magical places. On still days the ghosts floated alongside them, but Aunt Edna kept the golden cord looped on her belt, just in case the wind sprang up.

In the evenings, Isobel learned to wear the right diamonds for the right occasion. Tiaras for meals at the table. Necklaces for dressing up in Aunt Edna's old clothes. Bracelets and earrings for sitting on the veranda with the family. And sometimes, for no reason at all, everything at once which could be tiring. Diamonds were quite heavy.

The time flew by for Isobel and it was a week before Christmas when the delivery van arrived just as they returned from the morning's tree planting. The delivery lady came up the steps with two boxes. "For Mrs Edna Toddleby of Hopperfield Station," she said.

Aunt Edna took the boxes into the kitchen and opened them. There was a letter from Mr Hamble in one which simply read:

> "These are the last of the personal effects of Mr and Mrs Hopperfield."

One of the boxes contained a folder of papers, some jewellery and a photo album. The other box contained a brass vase with a lid screwed down tightly. Aunt Edna said it was called an urn, and Isobel's Mum and Dad were in it. She undid the lid and Isobel looked inside. The ashes looked like grey dust to her. It wasn't anything like her Mum and Dad and made her feel sad. They put the lid back on.

Aunt Edna and Isobel sat around the table with the ghosts and looked through the photo album. Isobel had never seen it before. There were photos of her as a baby and a toddler and one taken at her school just a few months before her Mum and Dad had died. Only one photo was of her with her parents. When Aunt Edna commented on that, Isobel said, "They travelled all the time. I didn't see them that much."

"That's a pity," Aunt Edna said sympathetically.

"I wish I could have seen them one more time. Just to say goodbye."

"Never mind, dear. You have this photo of the three of you together. You can keep that in your bedroom if you like. Next to your bed. That way they will be the first people you see in the morning and the last people you see at night."

Isobel liked that idea. She turned a page in the album and pointed at an old black and white photo. "Who is that?"

Aunt Edna peered at the photo and said with surprise, "Why, it's my brother, Thomas! Ma, Pa, come look at this."

Thomas was wearing baggy shorts and a loose shirt. He was standing with a rifle over his shoulder and a small boy next to him.

Pa said, "That must be his son. Look, it says 'Thomas Hopperfield Senior and Thomas Hopperfield Junior' under the photo. That's your grandfather and your great grandfather, Isobel."

Ma said, "Thomas is quite young there. Must have been taken in Africa."

They turned the page. Another old photo showed Thomas with a pretty lady and the boy who was a bit older.

Aunt Edna said, "That must be his wife. And to think we didn't even know he was married." There was a sorrowful shaking of ghostly heads all around the table.

On the next page was a photo of Thomas Junior as a teenager standing next to a gravestone. Bert said, "Look, you can see the names on the gravestone. Thomas died and so did his wife. Poor Thomas Junior. He was an orphan and we didn't even know."

The next photo was of Thomas Junior as a young man. It was his wedding photo and they could see the Sydney Harbour Bridge in the background. Granny said, "He'd moved to Australia. Why didn't he come to see us?"

Aunt Edna said, "Perhaps he didn't know about us. Thomas never was much of a talker. Perhaps he didn't get around to telling his son about Hopperfield Station." She sighed deeply. "Such a pity, but there it is."

They turned a page and there was Thomas Junior as an old man with a young man, young woman and a baby. Isobel gasped and said, "That's my Mum and Dad!"

Aunt Edna smiled. "Then that must be you when you were a baby, dear." She saw Isobel's sad face and took the photo out of the album. "We'll put this in a frame and hang it on the wall with all the other family photos. In fact, we'll put all these old photos in frames and hang them."

Grandpa said, "Edna, you must get a photo of you and Isobel to put up on the wall."

"What a splendid idea! We'll have to go into town and find a camera."

Isobel perked up a little and said, "I can take it. I can take a selfie."

Aunt Edna said, "What's a selfie, dear?"

"I'll show you." Isobel ran to her room and dug around in her suitcase for her mobile phone. She hadn't even thought about her phone until now. There had been so much other stuff to do and there was no one to ring or text anyway. She turned it on. There was no signal, but it was still charged and the camera worked. She ran back to the kitchen. "Stand next to me, Aunt Edna." They stood side by side and Isobel held the phone out in front of her and clicked.

They all looked at the photo and Isobel gasped. "Look, Ma and Pa are in it, too!"

Aunt Edna said, "What a clever little camera. Ghosts don't usually show up in photos."

"It's not a camera, Aunt Edna. It's a smart phone."

"It certainly is smart for such a baby phone. But how do you get that little photo out of it into a frame?"

"We send it to a printer."

"Oh. I'll have to ask Gerald at the Post Office. I think he's got one of those printery things."

"Can we get one of our own? I'll need it for school." Isobel held the phone up again. "But there's no signal. No internet. I need the internet for school. I do my homework on my laptop."

Aunt Edna shook her head. "Signal? Internet? Laptop?"

"It's alright. I'll explain it all later. But for now, everyone gather around and smile for another selfie."

The ghosts hovered behind Aunt Edna and Isobel, everyone smiled, she clicked and they all bent down to examine the photo. Aunt Edna exclaimed, "Why, that's perfect!"

Isobel said, "I need to charge my phone."

"Charge?"

"Plug it in. Before it runs out of power."

"Oh, I see. You can plug it in next to the fridge. Goodness, my broccoli and caramel biscuits must almost be ready." There was a WOOF and the oven door opened with a clang. "Just as I thought. Come on, dear, put your Mum and Dad on top of the fridge and we'll have morning tea."

As Isobel reached up to put the urn on the fridge, Aunt Edna said, "I wonder why your dear Mum and Dad didn't have their own separate urns?"

Isobel said, "Mr Hamble told me it was cheaper to mix their ashes and fly them home in one urn."

"Cheaper? Goodness, that won't do. That won't do at all. Cheaper is no way to treat a Hopperfield."

"I don't mind, Aunt Edna. I like to think of them together."

"Well, there is always that, isn't there? If you don't mind, then I don't mind. Put some ice in the jug of lemonade, dear, and bring it outside."

It was cool and breezy under the old pepper tree. When they had finished morning tea, Aunt Edna said, "You stay here while I get some washing out of the machine."

Isobel sat and enjoyed the warm morning. Summer holidays were the best. Her old life in Sydney seemed like a dream now. She listened to the magpies warbling in the pepper tree above her head and jumped when one of them suddenly screeched. There was a plop next to her and she heard a squeaky chirp.

Isobel looked down. A baby magpie had fallen out of its nest. It didn't look hurt. Instead, it opened its pink mouth and squawked for its mother. Isobel bent down and lifted it up. It was a fat little thing and didn't have many feathers on it yet. She knew there was no way it could fly back to the nest.

She looked up into the tree, but she couldn't see the nest. It had to be up there somewhere.

She had never climbed a tree. Her old school had not allowed such things. There were many branches. It looked like a good climbing tree to her.

Isobel tucked the baby magpie gently inside her t-shirt and started to climb. It was like climbing a ladder and much easier than she thought. She made her way upward, looking for the nest. She found it halfway along a branch leaning over the roof of the house. The mother and father magpie were perched next to the nest, warbling away as they watched Isobel. She sat on the branch and slowly worked her way along it. There were two more baby birds in the nest, their pink mouths open, waiting to be fed. Isobel lifted the baby magpie out of her t-shirt and popped it back into the nest.

She looked down. It was a long way back to the ground. She wriggled backwards until she reached the main trunk, grabbed a branch and slowly lowered herself down. It was fun. She kept going and reached the ground safely. When she sat down again, she felt very pleased with herself.

When Aunt Edna came out of the house with a basket of washing to hang on the line, she said, "Alright there, dear?"

"Sure, Aunt Edna, just fine."

Isobel looked up into the tree and decided to climb it again in a few days. She wanted to see how the baby magpies were getting on.

CHAPTER 15

A Gift from the Lightning Rock and a Northerly Breeze

Isobel had tea and cake on the front veranda with her family that night. The afternoon breeze had gone and it was very still. The stars were appearing in the darkening sky and the night birds had come out to sing. It was very peaceful.

Isobel was just beginning to feel tired and thinking of going to bed when she heard a rumble and felt a shudder under her feet. Aunt Edna looked up. "That feels like the Lightning Rock. Curious. I haven't called up a storm. Better go see what's happening."

They all went around the back of the house and looked up. The sky was changing to a purplish-pink colour and dark clouds were forming over the rock. Flash after flash of lightning lit up the sky. Aunt Edna said, "Something is up." She started to walk towards the rock.

Isobel put her foot out to follow, but could not move. She felt like she was standing in thick jelly and her feet were stuck. She called out, "Aunt Edna! I can't move!"

Aunt Edna stopped cold and turned around. She came back. "Show me."

Isobel put her foot out again, but she couldn't move it more than a few inches.

Aunt Edna said, "Are you sick, dear?"

"No. I feel good."

"Hmm. This is new."

The ghosts swirled around them. Ma said, "Try going backwards."

Isobel stepped back and found she could move easily. She stepped forward and got stuck again. Aunt Edna frowned and said, "Very curious indeed."

Grandpa glanced back over his shoulder and suddenly said, "Look. Look in the kitchen."

Isobel and Aunt Edna looked through the window. There was something glowing in the kitchen. The urn holding Mum's and Dad's ashes on top of the fridge was beginning to shimmer a bright gold colour. It got brighter and brighter until it shone like a light bulb. Isobel said, "Is it burning?"

"Let's go see." Aunt Edna raced inside and put her hand up to touch the urn. "It's cold." She took the glowing urn down and it began to pulse. "Goodness, it's alive!"

The urn began to rock around in Aunt Edna's hands. It rocked and rocked and suddenly broke free. It shot across the room towards Isobel who put her hands out to catch it. She held it and it stopped rocking. She said with some alarm, "What's happening, Aunt Edna?"

"I don't know, dear. Let me think. You couldn't walk forward, but you could walk back into the house. The urn didn't like being with me, but it likes being with you. Your Mum and Dad want something, that's for sure. And there's a storm on the Lightning Rock." Aunt Edna pursed her lips as she thought about it. Her cheeks puffed in and out, her eyebrows went up and down. Then her finger came up. She had an idea! She said, "Try leaving the house again with the urn, dear."

They all went outside and Isobel stepped off the back veranda. This time, nothing stopped her. In fact, she felt the urn pulling her forward.

Aunt Edna was looking at Isobel curiously. "Did you do anything today, dear? Anything different?"

"No. Not especially."

"Tell me everything you did."

"We planted trees. We opened the boxes from Mr Hamble. We had morning tea. We went for a swim. We rode out to the western paddock. We had sausage and caramel pie for dinner. I put a baby magpie back in its nest..."

Aunt Edna gasped. "I didn't see you do that."

"When you were getting the washing out of the washing machine this morning. It fell out and I climbed the tree to put it back."

Aunt Edna looked up at the tree. "This old tree?"

"Yes."

"How far up did you climb?"

Isobel pointed to the big branch hanging over the house. "All the way up there."

Aunt Edna gasped again. "That's a long way up. A long way..." She slapped her knee. "I know what's going on! You've been giving something to this country when you help me plant the trees, but that was my trade with the Lightning Rock, not yours. Today, you did something very special for the country. You saved a little bird. And now I think the Lightning Rock has a gift for you."

"Really? What?"

Aunt Edna pointed to the urn. "Something to do with your Mum and Dad. Let's go find out. It's a still night. We can all go. Come on!"

Aunt Edna strode away and Isobel ran to keep up with her. The urn felt warm in her arms. She liked the fact that her Mum and Dad were in it. She almost felt like they were really with her.

The ghosts floated ahead of them and were waiting at the top when Aunt Edna and Isobel reached the top of the Lightning Rock. Diggidydog and Grumblebumkin came up behind them.

The storm was in full throttle. Lightning bolts hit the big black rock every few seconds and the sound was deafening. The ground under their feet shook with every strike. There should have been wind, but there was none, only bolt after bolt of searing white lightning. Aunt Edna held Isobel's hand and yelled, "Let's wait and see what it wants!"

Isobel felt the familiar tingling in her fingers and looked down. Blue sparks began to shoot from her fingers. And then the urn jumped from her arms and floated toward the Lightning Rock. Isobel reached out to pull it back, but Aunt Edna yelled, "Let it go!"

The urn floated to the middle of the rock and began to spin. Slowly at first, then faster and faster. Suddenly, the three pronged blue lightning struck and everyone jumped, even the ghosts. It struck again and the lid of the urn spun off and disappeared up into the black storm cloud above them. The ashes inside the urn shot upward in a stream and formed a shimmering silver mist underneath the black cloud.

Then a different kind of lightning struck. It had four prongs and it was bright green. It hit the Lightning Rock with such a roar that Aunt Edna's teeth shot out and, as she caught them, she said, "Now, that's different." She popped her teeth back in, but it took a moment for them to stop rattling.

They looked on as the ashes started to slowly float back down to the rock. Another bolt of green lightning struck and the ashes glittered and shivered and took shape. Two figures appeared and Isobel thought they looked familiar. Then she gasped. It was her Mum and Dad!

Another bolt of green lightning hit the rock and this time it did not stop. It danced around the two figures and as it did, Isobel's Mum and Dad walked slowly to the edge of the rock. They looked just the way they had last time Isobel had seen them. Mum was wearing jeans and a blue top and Dad had his grey jacket on. They were transparent, like the ghosts, but even more so. They were barely there and Isobel was afraid they would disappear any moment.

Isobel was scared. Then she felt Aunt Edna's hand holding hers and she knew she would be alright. There was nothing to be scared of as long as Aunt Edna was with her. She raised her hand and waved at Mum and Dad. They waved back. They could see her! Then they both put their hands over their hearts and blew her a kiss. The kisses floated across the rock and Isobel felt them caress her cheek. There was so much love in those kisses that it warmed her all the way through. She blew a kiss back and called out, "Hello, Mum! Hello, Dad! I love you, too!" Mum and Dad waved again and began to float upwards. Isobel knew they were leaving. She called out, "Goodbye, Mum! Goodbye, Dad! Goodbye!" They waved again and suddenly the green lightning sucked them up and away into the black cloud.

They were gone. A stream of grey ash began to trickle down from the cloud into the urn, the lid followed it, screwed itself back into place and it was over.

The lightning stopped and there was silence. The black cloud shrivelled up and disappeared and the sky was full of stars again.

Isobel and Aunt Edna stood still, their hands entwined. The ghosts gathered around and Isobel could feel their presence. Diggidydog and Grumblebumkin rubbed against her legs.

Aunt Edna looked down at Isobel. "Alright, dear?"

Isobel was trembling. "Yes. I think so."

"Not too sad?"

Isobel took a deep breath. "No. I feel better. I saw them one last time."

"You did indeed. That was a very special gift the Lightning Rock gave you."

"It sure was."

"What would you like to do now?"

"I don't know. Maybe put the urn back on the fridge?"

"What a good idea."

"It will remind me of them."

"It certainly will."

"Should we bury them with Frozen Bert and give them a headstone?"

"That would be proper for a Hopperfield. But the fridge is a good place for now."

Isobel smiled. She'd had an empty space in her heart and now it was not empty. She was happy.

Aunt Edna said, "Would you like some broccoli and tuna ice cream when we get home, dear? A special treat for a special occasion?"

"Yes please."

"Excellent. Come on, we'd best be getting back..." Aunt Edna didn't finish the sentence. Instead, she cocked her head to one side, looked up at the sky and frowned a little. She licked her finger, held it up and said, "Uh oh."

"What's wrong?"

"There's a breeze and it's coming from the north."

"Is there something wrong with that?"

"Only if there's a Red Snow Storm with it."

"Red Snow Storm? In summer?"

"It's what we call a big dust storm. When it's from the north, it can carry red dust from the centre of Australia. And visitors."

"What visitors?"

Aunt Edna smiled knowingly. "Vampires, dear. But don't worry, Diggidydog will give us plenty of warning." She looked down at the grinning Labrador. "Are they close, Diggidy?" The dog looked up at her and shook his head. "Good. We have time to prepare."

"What do we have to do, Aunt Edna?"

"Well, for starters, we need to defrost some broccoli. A lot of broccoli. And we need to drink some strong broccoli tea."

"Why?"

Aunt Edna smiled a mysterious smile and said, "You'll see soon enough."

Isobel looked up at the sky and wondered what would happen next.

THE END
FOR NOW

This story will continue in
'AUNT EDNA and the FAT VAMPIRE'
Book 2 of The Aunt Edna Stories

Printed in Great Britain
by Amazon